D1616320

The *Secret* of
Multiplied Money

John Wolcott Adams

Published by Golden Key Publications
P O Box 30989
Phoenix, AZ 85046 USA

Books by John Wolcott Adams

Positively Alive!
How to Have 'Unexpected' Income
BE What You Are: LOVE
Thirty Days to a Better Life
Power Words for Prosperous Living
Prosper Now!
How I CAN Have Everything
Rev. John's Divine Love Plan
The Secret of Multiplied Money
Positive Prayer
NOW Power!

ISBN-978-0-9801676-3-4

PRINTED IN THE UNITED STATES OF AMERICA
10 9 8 7 6 5 4 3 2 1

Dedication . . .

This book is lovingly dedicated to Kathleen R. Fletcher. Thank you, Kathleen, for your years of friendship and loving support in so many ways, especially for your great prayer consciousness. I am grateful for you.

Acknowledgements . . .

My heartfelt thanks to *Marcie Scheffner* who so ably edited this book; to *Patrice Agliata,* graphic designer, (cre8design@cox.net) who graciously and expertly designed the cover of this book; and to *Janice Winscot* who did so much to help make this book come together. And to all of my prayer partners who faithfully keep with me in prayer for the many, many people who look to my ministry for spiritual support.

Contents

The *Secret* of
Multiplied Money

John Wolcott Adams

Introduction . . .

This book is about using money as seed and using the law of multiplication to manifest greater financial abundance. Although the title implies that it is only about money that is not wholly true. This book is really about getting more intimately acquainted with the Source of Divine Substance, and using the great energy of your mind to prosperize your life. Prosperize means to deliberately think and act in harmony with Spiritual Laws and Principles to produce a very prosperous condition.

Thinking is something you do. You can't help it. Money is something you use. When you use it as seed, you have the privilege of using your thinking to cause it to multiply. Read about the "Rabbit Effect" in Chapter 7.

1

Years ago I was given a copy of *Seed Money In Action* by Jon P. Speller, a New Thought minister in New York City. I talked with Rev. Speller a few times by phone and when I asked if I could use the book for a home-study course I was planning, he gave me permission to use the book in whatever way I desired. For several years, I offered my Seed Money home study course, which delighted and prospered students who participated. Some of the many reports of Multiplied Money, using the Seed Money formula, are included in this book.

I was impressed with the fact that I could actually "plant" money, speak my word for increase, and reap a tenfold return. Upon applying this formula, I was pleasantly surprised to learn that it worked, and I was delighted to begin receiving multiplied money!

At the time I was given the *Seed Money In Action* book, I was the assistant minister of Bremerton Unity Center in Washington State, and I was working to create a new Unity church in Port Angeles, Washington. Since I needed more money to support my family and the new church, the idea of multiplying my money had great appeal to me.

At first I gave very small amounts as I used the formula, which is called the Recipe in this book, and then gradually increased the amounts of money I planted. To my delight, I learned that the more I planted, the easier it was, and multiplied money came more easily and abundantly.

Faithfully using the Recipe for Tenfold Return, as instructed, I started planting money. I had quite a number of small and medium demonstrations. The big one came when, after living in a house near Bremerton for only three years, it was sold and I made a profit of over $6,000. That was quite a sum in those days.

Subsequently, I began teaching this amazing way to multiply money in classes and seminars in my own church and in other Unity churches in the Pacific Northwest. These classes and seminars were always well received and amazing stories came to me from very happy people who were financially planting and reaping.

Of particular interest, was a Real Estate lady who lived on Whidby Island in Washington State. She wrote to me several times to tell me of the financial blessings coming to her because of using the Recipe for multiplied money. One thing that happened was, although there was a downturn in the Real Estate Market at the time, her sales actually increased. Besides that, people seemed to want to *give* money to her!

In this book, I share with you the Recipe for multiplied money, plus other essential teachings I have learned that are essential to living a prosperous life. These give you a true foundation for multiplying your money and the understanding to create true prosperity consciousness.

There is nothing to stop you from turning to the chapter containing the Multiplied Money Recipe. However, I encourage you to read the foundational chapters first. If you just cannot help yourself and want to learn and use the Recipe for multiplied money, I won't blame you for reading that chapter now. Just be sure to go back and read everything else. By doing this, you will substantially increase your understanding and your ability to multiply your money and prosperize your life in a wonderful way. It will make your practice of multiplying your money even more successful.

This teaching will work for you when you persistently use it in faith as instructed. I will be grateful to hear of the results, so kindly write to me.

John Wolcott Adams
P O Box 30989
AZ 85046 USA

RevJohn@GoldenKeyMinistry.com

1

Quantum Prosperity

Part One - What is it?

It seems paradoxical that with so much abundance in the world, so many people still struggle to prosper. In some parts of the world, millions of people still live in poverty. While we should strive for peace, prosperity must be given high priority because it is extremely difficult for anyone to have peace of mind while struggling to adequately feed, clothe and house themselves. Collectively, we must do everything possible to help everyone to prosper, to abound in plenty, be abundantly happy and healthy, wanting for nothing.

Individually, we should do all we can to prosper in the way that God intends for all of His children. As Wallace D. Wattles pointed out in his book, *The Science of Getting Rich,* we should get rich because that is the best way to help the world. He said that it is not possible to live a really complete or successful life unless one is rich.

Further he stated that it is perfectly right that you should desire to be rich because it is not normal not to be rich.

It is time for us to accept the abundance of good God has for us, keeping in mind whatever we do for ourselves we do for others because we are all one. True personal prosperity is never selfish.

Of the many prayer requests I receive through my ministry, a large percentage of them are for financial increase. These requests are welcomed because prayer is the personal positive power that enables everyone to prosper. This includes you because you are always in the mainstream of universal supply, whether you are aware of it, or not.

So, what is *Quantum Prosperity?* How does quantum apply to prosperity? I will explain it in simple, understandable terms. It is really much simpler and easier than you might expect.

Quantum, according to the World Book Dictionary, comes from Physics and is a basic unit of radiant energy; the smallest amount of energy capable of existing independently. Light and heat are given off and absorbed in quanta. John R. Pierce wrote, "The Quantum theory tells us that light comes in little packages of energy called quanta."

I like that description because each of us, although not completely independent, is an amazing little package of light energy. It is the same energy that is inherent in all things and if everything were to change into its primary form, all would be light energy, which brings us to *mutation*. *Mutation* is the act of changing; change, alteration.

A Quantum jump is a sudden, spectacular advance; a major breakthrough. A Quantum leap is a great or major advance.

Are you beginning to see how quantum can be applied to prosperity? Most people, depending on how intent they are to prosper, do not want to fool around with a little more prosperity. They want it to spectacularly leap (major advance) to a much higher level, and they want it *now!* However, that requires a drastic mutation (change) in one's thinking process because everything begins in the mind.

While they may not think about it, people who play the lottery hope to take a Quantum leap into sudden wealth. The problem with that is that most of them have not changed their thinking, even a little, so they don't win. And, for those who do win, what they get often disappears rather quickly.

Prosperity doesn't mean the same thing to everyone, yet most people equate prosperity to having plenty of money. There is nothing wrong with having financial abundance, the more, the better. Jesus Christ, the greatest of Prosperity Teachers, never sanctioned poverty. He promoted prosperity, the abundant life.

Money, of itself, does not necessarily make a person prosperous. It is just a lot easier to live and be healthy with more money than not enough. The truth is, God wants you to have plenty.

There is no virtue in being poor and no one has a right to live in poverty. Poverty is a disease that must be healed, individually and collectively. As stated before, when you prosper yourself you add to the prosperity of all humanity. Therefore, it is right to be just as prosperous as you possibly can be – to be rich!

Quantum Prosperity requires a mutation or change—not just a slight or lukewarm change but a big change in thinking; a leap in consciousness which produces a totally different result. It involves your whole being—mind, emotions, body, life, and finances. It requires you to dramatically change how you think about yourself, your world— everything!

You are mystically made, sewn together by a spiritual thread throughout your mind and body which affects everything you do—the money you have, or don't have, your friends, health, happiness—all phases of your complete life.

Harmony is essential between your thoughts, feelings, body and finances in order for you to be totally prosperous, or to live the more abundant life. Accept nothing less. To accept less is out of harmony with the natural flow of universal energy.

A man, who had struggled for years to prosper, but failed, decided to find out why. When he did, he made a decision to *completely change his whole being*—how he thought about himself, his body, his life, and money. He took action to re-pattern his thinking and feeling, which resulted in a major advance—a Quantum leap in his personal prosperity.

What he did, you can do. In the following parts of this Quantum Prosperity chapter, I will address important points to help you take your own leap into Quantum Prosperity. Before reading further, determine just how prosperous you really want to be. What, exactly, constitutes your desired prosperity, and what you are willing to do to achieve your goal. What kind of service are you going to provide for humanity? Your definite decision is the first step in preparation for prosperity.

Golden Keys to Riches 'n Fun

FOCUS - There is power when you put your energy behind one idea. Scattered thinking brings scattered results.

DESIRE - You must have a burning desire for your goal to succeed.

COMMITMENT - Be willing to do whatever it takes. Once you decide upon a goal, make a commitment to achieve it.

PERSISTENCE - Keep going. You can if you believe you can.

ENTHUSIASM - It's contagious. Be a carrier.

KEY PEOPLE - Surround yourself with people who are doing the same thing you want to do. Be around wise people and become wise.

ACTION - Quality action produces results. Live your potential.

- Vonne Kjellin

Quantum Prosperity

Part Two - Preparation

In preparation for real prosperity, a good place to start is to examine where you are in relation to where you want to be in terms of the greater prosperity you desire. Take a really good look at what you think about most of the time. If you are not demonstrating abundance to your satisfaction, ask yourself why. There are often underlying causes that keep you from prospering. Sometimes people actually resist prosperity in the mistaken belief that it is beyond them or they should be more concerned with other things, so they give it a low priority while continuing to struggle to make money.

Here are a few questions to ask yourself: What do you think about yourself? Do you believe yourself worthy? Do you harbor angry, fearful, resentful, and/or guilt feelings? Do you suffer from a fear of lack? Do you spend time feeling sorry for yourself or worrying about from where or how you can get enough money to pay bills? Do you talk lack at all? If so, STOP! There may be other questions to ask yourself, so ask them. Really examine what is going on in your thought/feeling process and how you relate to everything. Pay attention. Listen to what is being revealed.

When you know what needs to be cleared from your consciousness, then release it with the understanding that it no longer serves you. Dedicate yourself to changing your whole belief system if that is what is required. This is an essential part of the mutation process. You do not have to change everything all at once. Determine to persist all the way. The good news is: changing even a small part affects the whole thus creating the mental environment that results in a Quantum Prosperity leap upward.

Resonance Repatterning is especially helpful in releasing old patterns.

It is very important to go within to the silence of your own soul and invite the Spirit of Truth to free you from all that might keep you from achieving what you really want. Then let the Spirit of Truth guide you in achieving your heart's desires.

Affirmations, such as the following, will help you to harmonize with, claim and accept prosperity. They will help you access the prospering Presence of God within you. Open yourself to this Presence, knowing that God is the source of your prosperity *now*. No waiting.

I release from my mind, heart and life, all non-prospering thoughts, feelings, and conditions.

I discipline myself to think, speak, and act prosperously.

God, in me, is my source and my prosperity.

Every day, in every way, I am growing richer and richer.

I give thanks for rich results now!

A young lady who got tired of the same old lack showing up in her life, decided to clean up and clean out all the mental stuff that had kept her from prospering. She stopped thinking and talking lack. Turning within to the Presence of God, she invited this loving, fulfilling Presence to prosper her. She then made her claim by boldly speaking prosperity affirmations, such as those above. She thought and talked prosperously. When others would talk lack, she would un-apologetically change the subject to something positive and prospering. Gratefully accepting God's riches as hers, this young lady's prosperity took a quantum leap that amazed her, not to mention the surprise of her friends! She had prepared herself to prosper.

You can do it too. When you prepare for prosperity, you become non-resistant to the great good you seek.

The basic law of prosperity is radiation and attraction. What you radiate outward in your thoughts, feelings, mental pictures and words, you attract into your life and affairs. - Catherine Ponder

Quantum Prosperity

Part Three - Nonresistance

Resistance is one of the biggest stumbling blocks to prosperity. A young man who was trying to prosper, but kept running into obstacles, found this out when he seriously asked why he didn't prosper. It was quite a jolt to his ego. When he sought the counsel and help of someone who could confirm it, he discovered that this was true. He immediately set about changing that belief pattern to align with the financial abundance he really wanted to resonate with.

People resist many things. It seems that we are taught to resist almost everything; to be careful not to get into areas where we might experience negative activity. Unfortunately, this same resistance movement is often carried into things that we desire.

The young man mentioned above, resisted forgiving himself for mistakes he had made and resisted forgiving other people for real or supposed wrongs. He had resisted letting go of things about himself that were no longer true, or of value. He discovered that he had spent a lot of time and energy in poor mouthing himself with endless talk of wanting prosperity, but always talking about the lack he was experiencing, and expressing all kinds of reasons why he probably couldn't prosper. He resisted giving up his practice of lack-thinking and talking, but was wise enough to realize he must if he really wanted to prosper.

Some people would rather fight than switch. They have strong resistance to giving up lack-thinking, anger, fear, and the belief they must struggle financially. The latter has usually become an ingrained habit that fights for its life when effort is made to change it. These people seem to get some kind of satisfaction from thinking and talking about how much they need to have more money while resisting the very thing they desire more of.

If you require professional help, get it. There are many good, reliable spiritual counselors and other practitioners available to help you. Ultimately, the best help comes from within you. Ask the Spirit of Truth to help you; to reveal to you what you are resisting and what to do to be free. You may be surprised at what comes to mind, but do not be dismayed. It has come to your awareness so you can release it and let it go. By all means, do not resist letting go. The same Spirit will help you do that.

To really prosper, practice nonresistance. This includes being nonresistant to forgiving yourself and others, and to accept the forgiveness of others. Add to this, being nonresistant to the Grace of God. Why is that? Because the Grace of God is His love for you over and above what you may seem to merit. In other words, in providing for you, God doesn't take into account what you have done or not done. He *will* provide for you, but you must jettison from your mind and heart the stuff that has blocked the receiving of God's rich good. Stop resisting what God wants to give you. When you do, you will discover you have made a Quantum leap upward toward the richer good you desire.

Affirm that the Grace of God is dissolving in you every negative condition—fear, anger, resentment, unforgiveness, guilt, and *resistance to the goodness of God.* By invoking the Grace of God, you cause a Quantum jump in the *quantity* and *quality* of your prosperity.

Many people resist being prosperous. With these people there seems to be a conscious or underlying resistance to money. It is a strong deterrent that causes them to struggle and it is hard for them to prosper.

A man desired to be abundantly prospered. He worked continually at providing a service that richly blessed many people, yet his own prosperity eluded him. Then, almost in desperation, he began a program of thought/behavior repatterning. He learned why his desired prosperity had kept away from him. Yes! It was resistance, plus other negative programming.

He not only resisted negatives, but he resisted prosperity, believing himself not good enough for it, especially having plenty of money. Since he was in spiritual work, his resistance took the form of: maybe it wouldn't look good if he lived prosperously. Yet, he knew at least one other person in the same line of work who was a millionaire.

Fortunately, he secured the guidance of an expert counselor in these matters and through the repatterning process, he was able to stop resisting, to let go of old baggage, and to let the money flow. And it did flow when he opened a space for his greater financial wealth to move into his life. He was now free to claim and accept the riches God had for him.

The true way of receiving greater prosperity is to refrain from resisting it. When you are truly receptive, you are like a city that is a great transportation center. Good things come to you from everywhere. But when you let your intellect tell you that your good must come to you in some certain way, you are very much like a town with only one road leading into and out of it. Everything you get has to come via that one road.

The law that governs water flow is often used by Truth teachers to help their students to understand how good is distributed. If a person becomes lost in the mountains, the best thing to do is to find a stream and to follow its downward flow. Water always finds the easiest way to the lowest part of the surface of the earth. That is why we have such large oceans.

Engineers make practical use of the fact that water seeks the easiest way down. Water never resists anything that may get in its way. It does not fight boulders; it goes around them. If the boulders are contacted by water long enough, the water dissolves them!

The way of nonresistance is the quickest way to receive your greater good, the good that God truly wants you to have and enjoy. You have an attracting power within you, a force that keeps your good flowing to you as naturally as water flowing downhill. Is there an apparent obstacle that may be keeping your prosperity from you? Unite your forces of good with the good forces that are seeking you. Dissolve the seeming obstacle by blessing it, by being willing to recognize it, not as an obstacle but as a possible means of bringing your greater good to you.

Let life flow. Let peace, joy, love, and money flow. Nonresistance is a golden key to Quantum Prosperity. Whatever you resist persists, so stop resisting.

We mistakenly believe that prosperity comes to us when we receive – when money comes to us or we get a new job. This is not true. Prosperity's demonstration is giving.

– Jim Rosemergy

Quantum Prosperity

Part Four - Love

*Love is the grandest healing and drawing
power on earth. It is the very reason for being.
Love is the sole impulse for creation.
The whole Universe is based upon it.*

– Ernest Holmes

If there is anything that will cause your prosperity to take a Quantum leap, it is love. Love is, far and away, the most powerful energy you can invoke or express for living prosperously. In fact, it is the only thing that can make your prosperity worthwhile.

People who desire greater prosperity will use affirmations, focus on the laws and principles governing prosperity, and on money. They will display great faith and confidence, too. All of these are good, however, love should be the main focus.

People who miss this point do not understand how love can be connected to their prosperity and they have no clue as to the need for giving love high priority. Unfortunately, their focus is on the "bottom line," which may be profit from a business, the stock market, money received from employment, or from sales. Again, these are all good, but they are results, not the cause of wealth. If love is ignored or focused in the wrong direction, then the prosperity path may be difficult and results meager and disappointing.

An important point to consider is your *love for prosperity*. It may seem odd but some people do not love to prosper. This may be due to a belief that to live abundantly—have plenty of money—is not spiritual. To prosper means to succeed, flourish, and to thrive. Therefore, it is in everyone's best interest to love prosperity, the more abundant life, because that is what God wants for all of His children. Jesus taught and demonstrated that we are here to live just as richly as possible.

Love is an integral part of prosperous living. When love is genuinely felt and expressed, it is never done for show or to impress others. Love is caring and sharing; being patient, kind, and understanding. While some wealthy people may flaunt their riches and status, there are those who unselfishly live life lovingly with the welfare of their fellow humans first in their hearts.

Politics aside, the Kennedy family is a good example of this. People usually respond to them with love and caring as demonstrated by millions of people when JFK Jr., his wife, and sister-in-law passed unexpectedly when their plane crashed into the Atlantic Ocean. When we love and care for others, it returns to us multiplied.

Of great importance is to love and accept yourself as deserving of the greater good you desire. Upgrade your self-worthiness, if necessary, and you will take a very prospering quantum leap upward.

Believe that God really can abundantly provide for you. God loves everyone unconditionally, withholding from no one. His loving provision is for all of us.

A woman struggled for years under a load of guilt believing that because of things she had done, she was not deserving of, and therefore not entitled to, a sizeable amount of prosperity. However, when she was helped to understand that God (Love) doesn't keep track of wrongs, she decided to fully and completely forgive herself, especially for denying God the opportunity to prosper her. Loving herself, she freely loved everything and everybody. Before long, prosperity miracles began happening to her. She was able to open her own business, which prospered in amazing ways because she filled her shop with love and loved everyone who entered her store. Later on, she reported that she had met a wonderful, wealthy man who was just as love-filled and loving as she was, and they were happily married. Yes, love causes quantum leaps in your prosperity, and in your personal relationships!

Love is great magnetic energy. When you focus on Love, you literally become a divinely irresistible magnet of all loving people, wonderful experiences, and divine substance in the form of money. Love is the name of the prosperity game. Love dispels fear and empowers your faith. Love is your great quantum energy for prosperity!

For your greater understanding and realization of the life-enhancing power of Love, please refer to the author's books, *BE What You Are: LOVE* and *Rev. John's Divine Love Plan – 52 Weekly Divine Love Inspirations.*

2

Substance

*All the Substance that ever was in material form
exists now, in some form. All the Substance that
ever will be in material form already exists
in some form.* – Ruthanna Schenck

Substance is always everywhere present. It is
what Carl Sagan called Universal Stuff. He said
everything is made of this one stuff. He didn't call
it Spiritual Substance, but that is what it is.
Charles Fillmore, co-founder of Unity School of
Practical Christianity, called it ether. He agreed
with scientists who said that the ether was charged
with electricity, magnetism, light rays, X-rays,
cosmic rays, and other dynamic radiations. He
said it is the source of all life, light, heat, energy,
gravitation, attraction and repulsion. And, it is the
interpenetrating essence of everything that exists
in whatever form on Mother Earth.

All of this is what Jesus Christ called the
Kingdom of God. He knew its great, all-providing
essence and this was the reason why he said,

"Seek first His kingdom, and His righteousness; and all these things would be added unto you."

This inexhaustible Substance is always present. This means that it is not only always available to you, but is the essence of your being. Because of its comprehensive quality, it provides for you the fulfillment of whatever you desire. The golden key is in learning how to access it. You do this by meditating in it, thinking in it, and through your spoken words that are alive with its power. When you speak, you actually speak your words into this all-providing, omni-present Substance. If you are wise, you will watch your words.

Substance is never depleted. It is always with you. You may depend on Substance to prosper you, because it is the foundation and essence of all wealth. Substance responds to your belief in it and your demands upon it. Substance is never affected by ignorant utterances of so-called hard times; however, if you give voice to a belief in hard times, your level of prosperity will be negatively affected.

Substance cannot be destroyed. Democritus, the Greek philosopher, said: "Nothing can never become something, nor can something become nothing." The word "destruction" should be taken out of the dictionary, because there is no such thing as destruction. Substance can be converted and transmuted, but it can never be destroyed. It may change form and often does, but it is *always* the same Substance.

While it is intelligent, thinking stuff, Substance has no choice but to respond to your beliefs and spoken words. Its nature is to give, to respond to your call upon it and it always does because it simply cannot help itself. This is another reason why it is much more profitable for you to watch your thinking and to listen to the words you speak. You are wise to think upwardly and optimistically and to speak accordingly. Refrain from thinking or speaking negatively, pessimistically, and most of all, angrily. This is another way of stating the Law of Attraction. You always draw to you that which resonates with your thoughts, feelings and words.

God is Substance, but this does not mean that God is matter. Matter is the out-picturing of Substance, which is unchanging, always perfect, always present. Matter, or physical form, is conditional while God or Substance is unconditional. Matter is a mental limitation of human belief.

Charles Fillmore said that Substance may be conceived as God-energy, or Spirit light. Physicist Sir James Jeans said that the material universe is made up of waves of which there are only two kinds: bottled up waves, which is called matter, and un-bottled waves, which is called light, or radiation. He said the process of changing matter is just the un-bottling, or releasing, of imprisoned wave energy.

More practically, this means that to make use of Substance, it is imperative to no longer believe that what you see is "reality," but the out-picturing of Substance. Jesus said to not judge by the appearance, but be right in your judgment. By this He was giving us the secret to changing undesirable circumstances and situations into desirable ones. He was saying that behind what you think you see is the always present, never-changing Spiritual Substance, and by changing your belief, and by speaking your word of faith, you can change appearances.

He knew this when He multiplied the loaves and fishes. If Jesus had only judged by the appearance, He would not have been able to do what He did. Instead He "looked up to heaven" which means to lift one's thinking and viewpoint. He had a keen realization of Spiritual Substance, which He knew was abundantly adequate to meet any need. Jesus called upon it to manifest according to his desire and the desire of the multitude to be fed.

Often the multitude can be very limited in their thinking. That is because they believe more in appearances than in omni-present Substance. They have a greater consciousness of lack and limitation than of unlimited Spiritual Substance.

While this is being written, the world is seemingly experiencing mass financial lack and limitation. This is made even more so by the news media; at least they make it appear to be worse than it really is. It would be interesting to see what would happen if a sufficient number of people would refuse to judge by the appearance and securely focus their attention upon limitless Spiritual Substance as the true reality and then speak their word of good and easy times of financial abundance; to speak upwardly and optimistically. I believe this would create a miracle like the world has yet to see, and could surely use.

Ideas

Substance is alive and overflowing with ideas. This is another reason for you to get intimately acquainted with Substance. No one should ever say that they are out of ideas. They should say they have closed their minds to further enlightenment. In the late 1800s, someone said the U.S. Patent Office should be closed because everything that could be invented had been. It's amazing how wrong he was! A better statement would be, "how unenlightened he was." He looked to appearances and didn't have a clue as to the fathomless workings of the human mind, to say nothing about creative, thinking Substance.

God is the real essence of Substance. This is true because God is all there is. That is why Substance is the reality of all that appears. It is what Jesus called upon whenever He performed so-called miracles. He had a keen realization of God as being the very Substance of life, of healing, and even turning ordinary water into fine wine.

Substance is that which stands under every visible form of life, intelligence, love, and power. All of this is within and around you and everything, every tree, flower, animal, your car and home. If this were not true, none of this could appear. Every drop of blood that courses through your veins is the free flow of Substance.

It is very much like the ocean. I suggest that you visit one soon and take with you a cup. Dip it in the ocean and fill it with water. In the cup you are holding part of the ocean. As you observe the water, accept that it contains all of the elements of the ocean. If you were to use other containers of varying sizes, they would all contain all of the elements of the ocean. The same would be true regardless of the size of the container you use. In other words, each contains the whole. The same is true with each individual manifestation of God. Each is the manifestation of God, the Substance that stands under all that appears. It is nothing less than Divine energy that pervades everything.

You are the highest manifestation of Divine energy, the most complete and magnificent expression of God. Being the highest creation, you have been given dominion over all manifestation. The way you exercise your dominion is through the intelligent use of your mind. In other words, you think, speak and act and thus cause whatever appears in your world, to be. This is another reason why you are wise to watch what you think and listen to the words you use.

No absence

There is no absence of life, substance, or intelligence anywhere. This is worth memorizing, to know with certainty that it is Truth. Of course, Life, Substance and Intelligence are invisible to the physical eye, because they are spiritual. Spirit cannot be seen, but it is *always* present.

One time I passed a street preacher who kept pointing at the sky when he referred to God just as though that was where God was. When I stopped and said to him that God was within him, he argued and said that he couldn't see God in himself. It was a cloudy day so I pointed to the clouds and told him that above the clouds there was blue sky and it was a very sunny day above the clouds. Unfortunately, he just scoffed at that idea and returned to his preaching, preferring to not be enlightened to the Truth of his being. I continued on my journey.

Some people are apparently content with wrong beliefs and wander around in the dark rather than open their minds to new ideas and illumination. Unfortunately, while refusing to think differently, they still expect different results. Substance does not work that way. It is intelligent and always gives to you according to your thought. If you want a better life, then you must better your thoughts because you are always thinking in Substance.

Faith

According to Hebrews 11:1, "faith is the substance of things hoped for, the evidence of things not seen." In other words, faith takes hold of the substance of your desires and causes them to become evident, or visible, in your life. That is why you are wise to put your whole faith into your practice of Multiplied Money. And everything else that is important to you. Then you can depend on the multiplying process to work for you. When you do, it works amazingly well!

It brings you satisfying results because you understand that when you speak your word of faith, you speak it directly into Substance. Thus you cause the invisible, but very present

Substance, to manifest according to your spoken word. Through faith you put clothing on your desires so are you able to see them with your physical eyes, and enjoy having them.

Again, God is the invisible Substance from which everything visible is formed. It is always surrounding you and flowing in and through you. This magnificent Substance that constantly surrounds you is unlimited and is the essence of whatever you desire. Its inclination and only work is to fulfill every claim you make on it. This is true for every need on Mother Earth. Spiritual Substance is capable of providing lavish abundance for every child of God and is always eager to do so. Wisely accept this as true for you and never again think or act as though there can be any kind of lack.

Substance always flows in at the center as it moves out into the manifest world each and every moment. It is an unchanging law that every one who asks in faith, receives. Asking is another way of claiming. This does not mean in the usual sense of claim, but through your spoken word (affirmation) of faith in omni-present Substance. I like to call this positive prayer in that you speak words of Truth (affirmations) in accord with the desires of your heart. Since Substance always responds to your call upon it, it must fulfill the desire you have spoken into it.

Substance is always totally present where you are, therefore, when you speak, you cannot help but speak into Substance. Being infinitely intelligent and responsive, Substance obediently takes the form and shape of your desires according to your spoken word.

You need not look for signs or wonders. If you think you must see flashing lights or other things when Substance is answering your call upon it, you will be disappointed. Substance doesn't work that way. It manifests itself quietly.

All you need to do is to be very still and accept in *perfect knowing* that your desires are being fulfilled, if not immediately, then a little later on. According to your faith, you will have the manifestation of the desires of your heart. You are wise, then, to quietly and firmly believe that God-Substance is at work, all is well, and your demonstration is made. Believe you have already received.

Gratitude

While this is more substantially addressed in another chapter, it is worthwhile to mention here that Gratitude opens and keeps open all the doors and avenues of supply. Therefore, it is good for you to speak words of thanksgiving toward the all-providing Substance within and around you in recognition of it hearing and responding to your faith in it. Thanksgiving lifts your thinking beyond doubt and creates a clear mental environment of trust and faith where you just *know* all is well and the whole Universe is pouring its wealth upon you.

If, at first, you are not aware of having received anything, do not waste time or energy in worry. You need not speak your word of faith again. Just continue to give thanks as you quietly listen and confidently wait for your desires to manifest while doing what needs to be done by you. It is important for you to know that your demonstration is made; you *do have* your heart's desire. Gratefully, trust the process. You never hear God at work, but He is. *Always!* Do not strain or be anxious. Be still and joyfully thankful and take whatever action you are guided to take. Perhaps, when you least expect it, your increase will appear. Bank on it!

Substance is God.

The substance, which we have been discussing, is actually God. It is wholly important for you to know this. Years ago, upon learning this Truth, I had to let go of old beliefs so I could accept this Truth. I would often declare, "God is not in the sky, God is within me." When I learned that God is Substance, then I made similar declarations so as to imbed in my consciousness the Truth of my being and of the Universe in which I live, and in which we all live.

It is important to never separate God and Substance. However, do not make the mistake of thinking that Substance is cold or unfeeling. In Truth God, Love, and Substance are one and the same, and always warmly comforting and all-providing.

Substance is limitless. In Truth, there is no beginning and no end of Substance. Therefore, it can never be depleted. It loves to be used and just because you are thinking in it and drawing upon it for the fulfillment of your desires, you do not diminish it whatsoever. Magically, or mystically, it rushes in, so-to-speak, to fill any seeming void. But, of course, there is never a void of Substance. You can totally depend on it, and you should. In fact, it desires, more than anything, to fulfill the desires of your heart. This is true whether or not your desires are good or less than good. You are wise enough to make sure all of your desires are of the highest quality because you get to live with what you cause to be manifested in your life.

Substance is alive creative energy, and is forever moving into the forms you and countless other people are making with your minds. That is because it is supremely intelligent, it thinks. Its natural impulse is toward more and more life, never less.

Thought is your power to produce tangible results, which are the result of thinking in spiritual Substance. Everything visible is made of this Substance. There is nothing else from which anything can be produced.

Do not judge by the appearance, but look beyond seeming limitations and so-called shortages and draw upon the unlimited Substance always available to you. The only thing required of you is to work in harmony with the spiritual laws and principles governing the manifestation of all the good things of life.

20 Substance Reminders:

1. All that appears is made from one Universal Substance.

2. Substance is intelligent; it thinks; it is alive and is Life Itself.

3. Faith or thought activity activates Substance. By impressing your thought upon Substance, the form of your thought is manifested.

4. Substance is always, everywhere present. Your mind, body, everything in and around you, and all that is, is permeated with, and *is* Substance.

5. You live in a friendly Universe of all-providing Substance of which you may have all you can use with abundance left over.

6. Substance is the foundation of your prosperity. Therefore you are required to look to Substance and not to channels. By living and thinking in all-providing Substance, you receive the magnificent abundance of God.

7. It is important for you to recognize Substance as the Source of all you need and desire, and to make your demands known to it. Otherwise, what you desire will not manifest in your life.

8. The Universe responds best when you believe you *already have* your desires, as though you own them now.

9. You do not need to pray for more Substance; you have all of it now! Pray for an expanded consciousness of Substance and for *the ability to receive more.*

10. Now is the only time. The Present is the only time for you to act in. (Refer to the author's book, *NOW Power!*)

11. Be absolutely clear on what you want. Have a clearly defined mental picture of your desires. In other words, have a definite Mental Equivalent of what you want. You cannot afford to be nebulous or hazy about this. Substance responds best to clear mental images.

12. Always let your vision be upon limitless Spiritual Substance, never on visible supply. Although you do not actually see Spiritual Substance with your physical eyes, you do "see it"

with your faith and imagination. Accept that riches are manifesting for you as quickly as you can appropriate them.

13. Spiritual Substance is pliable. You mold and shape with your mind—imagination—and it manifests in your life accordingly.

14. Look to and depend solely on Substance and you will be unaffected by recessions, hard times, or negative conditions.

15. Focus the great energy of your mind on, and completely cooperate with, Substance, and never talk failure, limitation, or loss.

16. Be totally honest with your fellow man. Through your own spiritual power, you create your own prosperity and help him create his.

17. Substance always responds positively to your creative thought and action and not to competitiveness. The Golden Rule is always best, creative, and prospering for you, and everyone.

18. Money gained competitively is always subject to loss. When you use the Recipe for Multiplied Money, you never compete with anyone for it. Your tenfold return comes directly from the Universe *through* infinite channels.

19. Money gained competitively is money de-manded from other people. It is lacking in love and creativity. Money received creatively, because of your creative action, comes because of what you

give. Always give more in value than you receive in money.

20. Whatever you desire, that is God desiring to express more fully in and through you. It is the natural expression of Substance taking the form and shape of your desire.

The game of life is the game of boomerangs. Our thoughts, deeds and words return to us sooner or later, with astounding accuracy.

– Florence Scovel Shinn

3

Thinking – Thought

Thought is creative. Thinking forms thought.
Words are the activity and embodiment of thought.

Thought is the power by which you create visible forms out of Substance. As stated before, Substance is that out of which all things are formed. That is why applying the Law of Attraction causes your desires to manifest in your life.

There is no way that the thought form of your mind can keep from being out-pictured. In a real sense, you are the originator of that which you experience. This is true because you are a thinking being. You are created to think. You thought yourself onto Mother Earth, thinking yourself being here, and eventually leaving.

One time, I saw a sign on a wall that declared: THINK! How unnecessary, because no one needs to be reminded to think. It is the natural action of your mind. The important thing is to make sure that what you think is in accord with the divine plan of the Universe, and your desires.

41

Thinking is the formulating process of your mind. It is your omnipotent I AM. Ideas flow through your thinking faculty. If only guided by the ego, thinking can be faulty, zealous, impulsive, and not always wise, but when guided by Spirit, it is sure and dependable.

You may have heard someone say, "I am a free-thinker." This is true for them, but it is also true for you and me and everyone. We all have freedom of thought regardless of what anyone else may think or say. It is God's gift to us. The key to happy consequences is in using our thinking faculty wisely and lovingly.

Thought is a product of thinking; a mental vibratory force. Thoughts are capable of expressing themselves. Thinking is the forerunner of words and causes ideas to be expressed. Both are vibrations that affect Substance. That is why you are wise to watch your thinking. Too often people allow their minds to wander around aimlessly thinking on things that may be detrimental to their health and prosperity. Since Substance responds to your thoughts, it is beneficial to make sure your thoughts are positive and uplifting.

Thinking is the action of the conscious mind; therefore, it can be unreliable. Yet, it is important because thinking is what we do most. It is important to know that you are always thinking in Substance, and that it responds unerringly.

There is a spiritual law which brings into manifestation the thoughts you focus your attention on. This is a divine universal law of mind activity that never fails. Although results may sometimes seem to come slowly, it doesn't mean that the law is not working, or that Substance is not responding. That is when you are wise to persevere and hold to your ideal. Your loyalty to Principle will cause the seemingly adverse condition to dissolve itself, and Substance will take the form and shape of your desires.

Never join anyone in entertaining "hard times" ideas. This kind of thinking is powerful to keep your desired prosperity away. People who engage in "hard times" thinking and talk, have a consciousness of lack and limitation. Get away from those kinds of people. Drive all thought of lack or "hard times" out of your thinking process. Remember, what you dwell upon in your thinking tends to manifest in your life experience. Flood your thinking with God-substance, the omni-present abundance that surrounds you, and soon this will manifest for you. This is adhering to the law of attraction and manifestation.

When you go to sleep at night is a good time to let thoughts and ideas of health, wealth, joy, peace, and abundance run through your mind. See them filling your home and the minds of everyone in your home. This activity of thought gives your subconscious mind right ideas for it to work on while you sleep. The result will be most satisfying.

Prosperity is always *for* you. Think on this. Believe it is true, because it is. Never allow yourself to feel unworthy. Remove all thought of yourself as "meant to do without." Think prosperity. Talk prosperity. Think and talk prosperity specifically pertaining to you. Make it personal. Accept that you deserve the abundance of good that God really wants you to have. Gratefully give thanks that it is yours now.

What is the quality of your thinking? You may know the quality of your thoughts by the quality of your life. If your life is not the most satisfying, examine your thinking, paying attention to your dominant thoughts. On the other hand, if your life is of high quality it is because your thoughts are of the best quality. Be advised, though, that the best is yet to be!

How determined are you to prosper? Some people desire to prosper, and they think very determinedly. However they have not overcome all doubts, and if their desired demonstration is delayed, as it usually is when doubt is present, the doubt increases until they may lose faith completely. What is needed is greater determination and persistence. You will persevere when you are strongly determined to succeed. Just remember to practice nonresistance. Go with the flow!

Through my many years of ministry, and in particular, teaching people how to multiply their money, it became apparent to me that the people who actually demonstrate real multiplied money are relatively few in number. They are the ones who determined in the beginning to prove the law of tenfold return for themselves and to persist in their quest. The others tried it for a while and if it didn't work for them real fast, they got discouraged, their determination and faith faded, and they stopped. Quite possibly, they had too many doubts to begin with, or couldn't allow themselves to really attract real prosperity.

The tenfold return Recipe works unerringly for those who use it in faith and who have a strong determination to have it work for them. Of course, some people are in the "try it" business. By this I mean, they will try many different things without really putting their faith in long enough to reap satisfying results. These people seem to just want to go from one thing to another hoping they will hit the jackpot without truly understanding the law, or doing the things that prosperity requires of them.

Optimism is paramount. If things seem slow in manifesting and worry tries to set in, determine that you will be patient. If negative thoughts tend to creep in, determine to be positive. In response to every thought of lack or need, renew your determination to prosper. Lift your faith and move forward.

Think in accord with what you want to experience. You are a thinking center and can create new thoughts, which you are always doing. Thinking prosperously in Substance gives it the form you want to produce.

While working with your hands is of great importance, the greater work is thinking. This is the creative process. Just like God thought the whole Universe and everything in it into manifestation, you think your desires into manifestation.

Writers and artists are good examples of this. They use their hands, but the books and masterpieces they produce are first in their minds where they think on and visualize them and their hands move accordingly. When guided by Spirit, the results are often amazing. The same is true with architects and engineers. The many beautiful buildings in the world were first ideas in their minds. The signers of the Declaration of Independence were visionaries. They envisioned a free land, governed by and of the people. Out of the minds of men and women have come great things, but it is also true of small ordinary things.

One day while I was studying at Unity School of Christianity, I had four questions to answer and get the paper and myself to class on time. Time was growing short and although I had answered three of the questions without much effort, the answer to the first question eluded me. As I sat in front of the typewriter, I got very still and quietly asked Spirit to guide me in answering that question. In about a minute or two, I "heard" a voice in my head that seemed to say, "put your fingers on the keys." When I did, I was amazed at what happened! I proceeded to quickly and easily write the answer to that question.

Having completed the paper, I rushed off to class and turned it in. Later, I learned that the answer to that question was excellent, and I received a very good grade on that paper. In those days, I didn't have the understanding I do now. I was pretty unaware of the thinking process, but I did have faith in it, and it worked for me.

The Truth is, no question you really desire an answer to will go unanswered. Intelligent thinking Substance always answers. When you ask the right questions, your *I A M* seeks and finds right answers. (See "Your Q Power", Chapter 15.)

James Allen wrote in *As A Man Thinketh,* "A man's mind may be likened to a garden, which may be intelligently cultivated or allowed to run wild; but whether cultivated or neglected, it must and will *bring forth.* If no useful seeds are *put* into it, then an abundance of useless weed-seeds will *fall* there in, and will continue to produce their kind."

What James Allen is saying is, your life experience is according to the thoughts you entertain with your mind. When you use your God-given wisdom, you tend your mental garden with care so as to weed out unproductive thought-seeds and take care of and positively nurture the thought-ideas you desire to see manifested as your life experiences.

This is especially true with your practice of money multiplication. When you sow money as seed, you sow with it the idea of increase, multiplication and enrichment, which are expressions of love. The Law works on more than just one level. Giving money as seed, you always give yourself what you truly are. This is why it is important to take care to weed out all lack-seed-thoughts.

Every thought-seed you allow to fall into your mind, and to take root, produces after its kind. Sooner or later, it bears fruit as an action or circumstance.

You do not attract that which you *want,* but that which you *are.* It is essential, therefore, to plant good thought-seeds in your mind so that you attract to you, desired life-experiences.

It is said that we may have a train of thought. A train delivers its cargo or passengers to a destination. Likewise, a train of thought delivers its creative energy into its outer form. If you direct your train of thought as a mental image of lack, it will always arrive at its destination as wrong concepts and ideas and your destination will be poverty station. Unhappy, impure, fearsome beliefs do the same thing.

You are wise, then, to make sure your thought-train is alive with positive, prospering ideas so that your train becomes the prosperity express and whizzes right on by poverty station as though it wasn't there. In fact, when your thought-train is alive and vibrant with creative, prospering ideas, it will destroy poverty station as it flashes by. Practice using the creative power of your mind for the construction of only images of the greater good you desire and see it manifesting as the fulfillment of what God wants for you.

Use your imagination

With your wonderful imagination, see yourself with your tenfold return. Imagine that you have it in your hands now. See yourself using it wisely as you lovingly share it with others. What will you use it for? Hold a picture in your mind of a new car, house, travel, or something very special that you have always wanted to do, have, or be.

Imagination coupled with faith is supremely empowering. Use your imagination to "see" your tenfold return coming to you. Place your faith completely in God – Infinite Intelligence – to bring about the fulfillment of your desires. Your work is to plant your money in faith, and let Infinite Intelligence provide the increase.

Feel you are successful

and prosperous,

since the feeling of

wealth produces wealth.

- Joseph Murphy

4

Don't "Swiss Cheese" Your Prosperity

Jesus said, "When you pray, believe you receive." He was stating a powerful prosperity principle and action of Mind. He knew that everything is done by faith. He also said to have the faith of a grain of mustard seed, which is very tiny, but carries in it enormous potential. What he was really telling us is this: We are to do as the mustard seed does and do not question, doubt, or have qualms about what will happen. Neither does the mustard seed bother with thoughts of unworthiness, past mistakes, or other stuff that tends to keep humans (the higher species) bound to lack and limitation.

When you think about it, what the mustard seed does, which is nothing, is amazing! It doesn't get in its own way. It never sabotages itself with negative, unproductive or demeaning thoughts and beliefs.

There is infinite potential in all seeds. (This includes money-seed.) They do what they are designed to do. The same is true with prosperity thought-seeds and idea-seeds.

When F. W. Woolworth started his first five and dime store, it was very small and people said it would fail. He proved them wrong. He was the one with the seed-idea and the faith. Things multiplied because that is the nature of God and faith thinking in infinite divine energy, omnipotent Substance.

The nature of our wonderful universe is to give forth of its Substance pouring it into our goals and desires which we formulate with the imaging power of our minds. How unwise it is, then, to set prosperity goals, begin with faith, and then allow doubts to ruin things and keep the good we desire from coming to us.

Don't "Swiss Cheese" your prayers or your prosperity. Swiss cheese has holes in it. When you doubt and fear, you poke holes in your faith and sabotage yourself and your prosperity. The same thing is done when you engage in lack thinking and talking.

Regardless of the shape of the economy, or what you have done or not done, now is the time to put your faith to work; to prove that you really do believe that God is not only adequate, but power-fully able to abundantly provide for you. The increased prosperity you desire depends upon your faith in God, in omnipresent Substance.

So hold your faith high. Give no thought to doubt or fear. Do not entertain thoughts or feelings of financial lack or limitation. Act as though you absolutely know the good you seek is coming to you and is yours right now. Do not question, do not doubt. KNOW it is so!

Do not wait; the time will never be "just right."
Start where you stand, and work with whatever tools you may have at your command, and better tools will be found as you go along.

— Napoleon Hill

5

The Fable of the Frogs

Once upon a time there were two frogs. One frog lived in a well and had never been out of it. One day another frog came upon the well, looked in and seeing the well frog called down to him and asked if he could come in. The well frog told him to come ahead. With that the other frog leaped down into the well.

The well frog asked his visitor where he lived and he said he lived in the ocean. "Ocean? What is that?" croaked the frog that lived in the well. The visiting frog said, "It is big, very big and it is not too far from here." "How big is your ocean?" asked the well frog. "Is it as big as this?" as he gestured toward the board he was sitting on. "Oh, it is much, much bigger," said the visitor. "Well, how big is it?" his host demanded to know. "The ocean is so big it would make thousands and thousands of this well," said the visitor frog. With that the well frog said, "Nonsense, nonsense, that is a lie, nothing could be bigger than this well. You are a liar and prefabricator. I want nothing to do with you! Get out of my well! Get out of my well!" And so, shaking his head, the ocean frog left.

The reason I have told this story here is to point out the fact that many people are like the frog in the well. They have created a very small belief system for themselves and are not willing to expand their thinking or their vision. If a well-meaning person tries to help them change their perspective, they sometimes become irate because it is upsetting to their deeply ingrained mental state. While they may say they might like to prosper, they are unwilling to change their viewpoint and to make the inner changes that are required. So, they remain in the old thought patterns and less than the best conditions.

This is most unfortunate because they are ignorant of actually living in a fabulously rich Universe that is teeming with Substance which is more than willing to enrich their minds and their lives. So they continue with their very narrow view of life unaware of the unlimited spiritual potential within them. Unwilling to change, they are not about to allow anyone to monkey with their beliefs. How unfortunate this is when they could live as the ocean frog does who is well acquainted with the unlimited abundant Substance.

As you read further in this book, open your mind to change. Be open to new ideas. Allow what is written in these pages to inspire you and expand your consciousness so that you catch the larger vision, the grander possibilities. The Universe is waiting.

6

Money is Wonderful!

If you are like some people, you may have believed that money is not very good. Some people tend to treat money as something to be avoided while doing all manner of things to get it! They chase after something that often avoids them, and then wonder why. If that is the case with you, now is the time to change these beliefs and behaviors.

Just like people tend to avoid those who speak despairingly toward them, money will do the same because money is alive with energy and responds to your thoughts, words and feelings toward it. To have greater amounts of money coming into your life, it is essential for you to love it. When I say to love money, I do not mean to love it for itself alone, or to worship it or to make a god of it. That is always wrong. What I do mean is to understand that money is formed of the same Substance as everything else, including your body, home, car, friends, and all things beautiful. Therefore, it is more than good and wonderful and deserves to be appreciated.

Contrary to popular belief, a very large number of people spend a lot of time thinking about money, how little they have of it and how they can get more; get enough to pay the rent or mortgage, for food, electricity, and so on. They think a lot about their lack of money. This is a waste of time and energy that can be put to better use such as thinking on and planting money as seed, thus claiming and receiving a tenfold return. In other words, a re-direction of thought is required.

One of the main reasons why some people have so little money is because of resentful, negative attitudes toward it. They are ignorant of money's intrinsic value. I don't mean the various denominations of money. Money is God's idea of circulation. It is God's good green energy, and does a tremendous amount of good when used wisely and lovingly. Money is a handy medium of exchange.

The practice of the Multiplied Money Principle requires that you focus on God, the Source, and to see money for what it is, an integral part of all that God has created for your use. Since God is everywhere, in all things, and is absolute good, then money is good. Lift your thought concerning money and you will open a larger space for it to bless you. And it will do so willingly and more abundantly! Always keep your main focus on God, the Source.

Money is God in action, or flow. In the grand scheme of things, money is important. Money is as essential as the clothing of your body, providing comfortable housing for yourself, for transportation, and enjoying the pleasures of life.

Money enables you to attend inspiring lectures and workshops and churches that feed your soul with Mystic Nourishment. It provides books, CDs, and DVDs for your enlightenment and soul growth.

Money also provides the materials for beautiful buildings, highways and byways, parkways and freeways. It is used for city, state and national parks for you to relax and hike in, and to renew your soul in.

Money, a lot of it, makes the Internet possible and helps all of us to keep in touch by e-mail and other modalities. Money is neutral in that it doesn't matter to money who uses it or how it is used.

That is why it is important to use money only for good and peaceful purposes. It is never good to use money for war, which is wasteful and never achieves something of lasting value, or creates peaceful conditions. The Golden Rule is most valuable when applied to money.

Using money as seed in order to multiply it in your life so you may enjoy more of it is an excellent use of money because you use it to bless other people. Just imagine how wonderful it would be if everyone used money in this way! We'd all be so busy giving to each other we wouldn't have time for selfish things.

Since money is neutral and alive energy and is for our free use, we have the responsibility of using it responsibly, which means wisely and lovingly.

It is important that you pay attention to your thoughts and feelings around money. Eliminate thoughts and feelings of lack and limitation, of hard times, of scarcity, of "hard to come by," anger, greed, guilt and resentment. Refrain from arguing about money with anyone. If you engage in this, you are both causing money to avoid you. It is better to seek for peaceful resolutions to all money disputes. This is love in action and always brings the best result for everyone.

Do not believe that anyone can cheat you out of money. If that seems to happen, it is the result of holding angry, fearful thoughts and feelings of loss. Stop believing in loss. No one can take away from you that which is rightfully yours, without your permission. If you hold thoughts and feelings of loss, anger and unworthiness, you radiate permission to others to show up to free you of your money. This happens, too, when you try to hold too tightly to money. If you do this, in a way, you are trying to squeeze the life out of it and as soon as it can, it will leave you. Tightly holding onto money is fear. Money just doesn't respond positively to fear, and will leave quickly, if it comes at all.

Remind yourself often that money is abundantly available; that it is God-Substance constantly flowing throughout the Universe. Therefore, more than enough is flowing freely, right where you are. Especially, do not think or feel fear in the presence of money. Think and feel love and money will flow in your life more abundantly. One day, while I was establishing the new Unity church in Port Angeles, Washington, the treasurer of the board called and expressed her worry about paying some bills. Several hundred dollars were needed. I said to her, "With all the trillions and trillions of dollars in the world, God can surely provide us with a few hundred dollars." She had thought about that, but wanted to be assured that the money would come, and it did.

Stuart Wilde wrote in his wonderful book, *The Little Money Bible*, "There are trillions of dollars zipping about electronically on any given day. Those electronic signals are literally passing through your body right now!"

This should give you a grander feeling of abundance and realize that there is plenty of money for you and for everyone. It is wise for you to think intelligently about money, but do not be indifferent toward it. Do not think about it in a dysfunctional manner. This stops the flow. Thinking about money in a loving, positive way enhances the flow and that is what you want. This is especially important when using money as seed, and it helps to multiply it.

Even Mother Theresa loved money in that she had a very good attitude toward it. While she busied herself with the magnificent work she did in helping millions of people and appeared to not care about money, she knew how to get it, and the Universe provided millions for her to use, not for herself, but to more efficiently and effectively do her work.

Of great importance is to believe you are worthy and deserving of an abundance of money and all the goodness of God. Negative, undeserving thoughts, feelings, and beliefs serve as roadblocks on the royal road to riches. They are just like traveling on a nice highway but discovering that someone dumped truckloads of big rocks on the roadway.

It is far more profitable to think highly of yourself, not in an egotistical way, but as the deserving child of God you truly are. You are nothing less than a deserving, useful, wonderful child of God. As a child of the Universe, you deserve the very best – in abundance!

It has been said that "money isn't everything" and it isn't. Money won't buy happiness, peace of mind, freedom or the good things of life.

Money is your friend. Make a friend of money and you will have many friendly get-togethers!

Many people struggle to get money. If you are one of them, stop! Struggle comes from fear and a belief in hardship: believing that money is scarce and you must put forth a great amount of effort to get it. If working hard were the key to riches, all hard-working people would be rich!

Napoleon Hill said to THINK and Grow Rich. He didn't say to work hard. Those he wrote about used their minds. Their creative mental activity created their wealthy conditions. Surely, there is a certain amount of physical effort involved, but hard labor is not included. If you've been struggling to get money, STOP! Relax. Let the money flow.

Think right about God, yourself, and money, and you will realize you *are* rich and then money will flow more freely.

Stay close to God in prayer. Relying totally on the Source, cease all struggles and money will flow more easily and copiously in your life. When I say to stay close to God in prayer, I do not mean that you must constantly ask God for what you want. Never beg or beseech God to prosper you. Begging and beseeching implies conscious separation from God and when this happens, the flow is cut off.

Staying close to God means to consciously practice the Presence all the time. It means to use positive words and prospering declarations of Truth. (See the Daily Declarations of Truth, Chapter 10.) Positive prayer* is affirming that God, you, money, and good are one. Remember, you live in the midst of Divine Substance, which is the energy that fulfills the desires of your heart. *Refer to the author's book, *Positive Prayer.*

To have plenty of money flowing through your life, develop a positive closeness with it. Instead of thinking of it "out there somewhere," think of it as always where you are. Remember, money is God in action and God is *always* where you are as intelligent Substance/Energy. Since money is a form of Substance, it is *always* where you are. The amount of it you have depends upon your consciousness. A consciousness of abundance attracts it to you in delightful quantities.

Money is God's good green energy! Having plenty of it is a good way to "go green."

Having a positive self-image creates a closeness to money, because money is positive energy and like attracts like. It is the Law of Attraction in prosperous action!

As good and wonderful as you are, it is never advisable to think of yourself as too good for money, or that somehow money is beneath you. This kind of attitude only causes money to avoid you. Remember that you and money are spiritual – made of the same God-Substance. Therefore you are good enough for money and money is good for you – lots of it!

Stuart Wilde said in *"The Little Money Bible,"* "You have a divine right to abundance, and if you are less than a millionaire, you haven't had your fair share. Even if you *are* a millionaire, there's nothing to stop you from acquiring more money. You can then use it to assist others and spread goodness and light." Give money as seed.

Think of money as "solidified love." Let money be a motivator of creative activity. Let it drive your creative juices which is another way of saying, let the love flow. Let it flow through your consciousness moving divine ideas out into expression. Thus, you are inviting creative ideas to fill your mind and manifest in your life as lovely new things and experiences.

Make multiplying your money fun. Be serious about it, but make it a game – a game you enjoy! Go about it lightly.

Money is unconditional in that it comes to whoever wants it and attracts it. Money may be used by anyone for any purpose. It doesn't care who or what. Its main purpose is to be used, to do good and to flow abundantly.

David Cates wrote in his book, *Unconditional Money*, "Most of us do money backwards. We believe abundance will come if we work hard, spend wisely, plan, save, and invest. That method rarely brings abundance. At best, it brings survival.

"I've never really let my money flow because I treated it with fear and caution. I've never experienced unconditional money because I've never dropped the masks and put myself out on the line.

"Unconditional money, like unconditional love, means living free from expectations and conditions. It is a vast and profound allowing in which life becomes a partner in the process, not an adversary or distant god.

"The truth is there are a million ways to create love and money, a million ways to fly your dreams and live without limitation. It doesn't take a lot of clout or power to play your own tune. It just takes a lot of courage and nerve.

"Money flows through any channel you let it. So does love, and joy, and freedom. Every part of you has infinite creative power. Let life do its work."

Get used to the idea of having plenty of money. You are working on multiplying your money— expanding the measure of money flowing through your life, so act as though it is already so.

This doesn't mean to go off on an ego trip because if you do, you will surely trip and fall – all over yourself! It does mean to have a solid conscious connection with God, the Source. Every time you use money, remember that it is a symbol of wealth, not wealth itself. It is God in action. Let it remind you that you and God and money are one and the same.

In other words, let using money be a spiritual experience. Let this especially be true when paying bills so that you do it joyfully with love and gratitude knowing the whole Universe is pouring more Substance in upon you and your money is never depleted.

By all means, never refuse money. If someone offers to buy your dinner, let them! Thank them and the Universe. If someone wants to pay you for doing something for them, graciously and grate- fully accept! If they do not pay you, be sure to make your tenfold claim on the value of your gift to them.

Money doesn't make you secure. The only thing that can make you feel secure is your conscious connection with God, the Source. God is love and when you are consciously connected with God you are not only connected with love, you know that you *are* Love. Using money as seed is acting compassionately toward others. It is love in expression.

When you think about it, money really is wonderful and when you have plenty of it, it is even more wonderful!

You can have everything in life

you want if you will just

help enough people get what

they want. - Zig Ziglar

7

The Secret of Multiplied Money

The Prosperity Laws of Attraction,
Tenfold Return, and Sowing & Reaping
Practically Applied.

Learn to multiply your money tenfold
and reap a harvest of Multiplied Money.

Using Money as seed, in faith, believing, is a practical and scientific method that works perfectly to increase your money tenfold when you follow the Recipe for Multiplying Your Money in faith.

This Recipe is Scientific and has been used by very wealthy people to create and increase their financial fortunes. Do not dismiss this method until you have sincerely practiced it for at least 90 days. It is the Law of Sowing and Reaping and the Law of Attraction practically applied to your money. The best part is, IT WORKS!

Follow the proven recipe of "Planting" money for reaping Multiplied Money. It's simple, but understandably, some people are skeptical. When they learn why it works, and begin to reap the benefits even a little, all negatives disappear. They become believers and rejoice as their money multiplies before their eyes. Read the following letter from a believer in Georgia, USA.

"Since beginning to "plant" money, per the Recipe, which I found to be extremely helpful, my understanding of this prosperity principle has increased. I am happy to report that I have received over $1,000! This is more than a tenfold return on money I "planted." Needless to say, I am delighted with my practice of Multiplied Money and how it works. Thank you for teaching me this valuable method to multiply my money and increase my prosperity. I am enclosing my grateful tithe plus more money I am seeding."

NO Risk!

One of the things for which money can be used, and which is not generally known, is as Seed. Just as you plant a seed in the ground and you reap a multiplied harvest, so it is with seed money. Many happy people understand that money can be given away and produce a tenfold return without any risk whatsoever. The Law of Tenfold Return *always works*. When you follow the Recipe, as prescribed in the next chapter, there is absolutely no risk whatsoever. The Principle of Multiplying Money is infallible. It's just like making a cake. When you follow the recipe, the cake turns out beautiful and delicious. You are happy with the result.

If you do *not* follow the recipe precisely, there is risk because you are not actually using your money according to the Principle. However, what is true is: *It works perfectly when you perfectly work it.*

The principle of aerodynamics never fails to work when a plane is constructed properly and is operated in perfect harmony with Principle. The Principle of Money multiplication works in the same way. If the Principle isn't applied properly you are not working the Principle. You are not gambling when you plant money as seed according to the Recipe. Using money as seed is a scientific way to multiply your money. It is a mental/spiritual activity that directly affects your finances in a very positive and prospering way.

Belief is the key!

If you think you *may* receive a tenfold return from planting seed money - you won't. When you follow the Recipe and *believe* you receive a tenfold return from your Seed Money -- you *will*. *Belief is the key*. There is no room for doubt. *Believe* you receive. Ask and it will be given you. Seek and you will find. Knock and doors of abundance will open for you – doors to vast universal riches! Jesus said, "What things you desire, when you pray, *believe* you receive them, and you will have them." He didn't say that you *won't.* He didn't say you *might.* He said that you *will. According to your faith is it done unto you.*

Ruthanna Schenk wrote: *"When you have both good eyesight and good mind-sight, you will see the abundance about you and you will believe in it. When you believe in it you will have mastered the first step in getting it."*

Do not give others permission to keep your good from you.

Too often, someone will allow another person's doubts to keep them from reaping the benefits of their efforts. These well-meaning, but misinformed, people scoff at what someone may be attempting to accomplish. I call this the ice-water effect. That is why I often advocate being very quiet about your goals, keeping them close to your heart as you move forward in your endeavors. Often secrecy is the best policy. This is usually true when embarking on using money as seed, expecting to reap your tenfold return.

When I first began to learn and to practice using money as seed, I had enough to do to contend with my own doubts and fears, let alone listen to those who knew nothing about what I was doing. You are wise to not talk to anyone about using money as seed unless you absolutely know they will agree with, and fully support you. Pay no attention to doubters and scoffers. Just be quiet, plant your money, believe and give thanks as though you have already received, and let the multiplied money roll in.

A man wrote me to say: "I've been practicing seed money for a few weeks with some rather small results. The problem seems to be with one of my buddies who scoffed at the idea when I told him about it. This caused me to have some doubts of my own. What should I do?"

I wrote back to this young man and encouraged him to renew his faith in the planting and reaping process, to KEEP QUIET about what he was doing, and be grateful just as though he was already receiving his multiplied money.

In a few weeks, he wrote back to me to report that he was following my suggestions while continuing to quietly plant money as seed. Within only a few days, after planting $10, he received $120 from a totally unexpected source. This was followed by larger tenfold returns as he began to plant larger amounts of money. When his buddy wondered why he seemed to suddenly have greater income, this young man then told him what he was doing. Needless to say, his buddy was curious and wanted to learn how to do the same, and was soon reaping multiplied money for himself.

Not long after presenting my first seed money seminar, a student who attended only the last portion of it wrote to tell me what happen when she began to plant money and make her tenfold claim as instructed. Here is what she said, "Today I received $320! I had accepted a job on a volunteer basis and planted my first seed money in the amount of $10, which I gave at your seminar. Right after beginning my work as a volunteer, the organization decided that the position would be salaried. Two weeks later, I received my first check. I know that belief is the key. When there is belief, there is a letting go, a release and expectancy."

This young person quickly grasped the idea. She proved in a wonderful way, the marvelous prosperity-producing principle in using money as seed. She did as instructed, prayerfully believed she had received, put the substance of her faith in what she was doing and moved in the right direction. She incorporated the law of sowing and reaping and her seed came back to her, "pressed down and running over".

Shortly after this student first wrote to me, she wrote again to say, "I just received an unexpected grant of $150 to be applied toward my tuition. Now I plant money daily." This lady was very fortunate to learn the Secret of Multiplied Money at a young age and not have to deal with doubts and wrong ideas about money as life progressed for her.

Although we are talking about the use of money in this book, it should be clearly understood that we are really working with a principle and right attitudes of mind. The gaining of great wealth should not be the object of this practice. If you enter into it with the idea that just accumulating lots of money, just for the money, you may be disappointed.

You will have lots of money when you seed it and make your tenfold claim because as you work in harmony with principle, the natural result is money coming to you more abundantly. The real object of using money as seed is to work with the spiritual laws and principles of prosperity; to grow your consciousness; and to enrich your awareness of God as your instant, constant source of supply. Also, it is important to take hold of Spiritual Substance with your mind and establish your faith securely in it. This is what ultimately causes multiplied money to flow more fluently in your life.

Fear closes -- Faith opens
doors of Abundance.

Some people, who learn the Secret of Multiplied Money and attempt to apply the Law of

Tenfold Return, fail because of fear. Fear is a big block to demonstrating the increased wealth you desire. Fear of loss stops the flow of Spiritual Substance-Energy. It closes the avenues through which this all-providing Substance-Energy flows, and causes you to feel separated from God, the source of all wealth.

The Law of Tenfold Return is based on faith – absolute trust in God, in the understanding that God is the Omnipresent Substance-Energy that takes the form of your multiplied money. When you have complete faith and trust in God, you cannot fear.

The "Rabbit Effect".

The Practice of Seed Money requires your complete faith and trust in God as the all-providing, always-present Source of all your good. Delete fear from your thoughts, feelings, and actions. Have complete and full faith in the omnipotence and omnipresence of God to provide richly and abundantly for you. Never question God's ability to give you His riches. Absolutely know that "all that the Father has" is yours now and always. As you do this, the doors of abundance will open wide for you, creating what I like to call the "rabbit effect," magnificent blessings that multiply and multiply!

8

The Multiplied Money Recipe

*Instructions for "planting" money
for the purpose of making your tenfold claim.*

1. "Plant" any amount of money by giving it to another person, group, or organization for any good cause.

2. Immediately after doing so speak these words several times: "*I have received* (ten times the amount given) *in return with good to all concerned. Thank You! Thank You! Thank You!*" For instance, you give $10 to a friend. Declare: "*I have received $100 in return with good to all concerned. Thank You! Thank You! Thank You!*"

3. Release it in love and give no more thought to what you have done except to feel good about it, and move forward in confident expectation and joy just as though you *have received* your multiplied money.

4. *Act as though it is already so.* In Truth it *is* already so. When you make your tenfold claim,

your multiplied money is yours NOW! Do not think of it as a future thing, but as a NOW thing.

5. If any thought of lack comes to mind, declare several times with power and joy: "I HAVE! I HAVE! I HAVE!" This will drive all thought of lack out of your consciousness and fill it with thoughts of abundance.

Emmet Fox wrote: "The verb *to have* is a part of the verb *to be*. In the very ancient languages there is no verb *to have*. It is a modern improvement, like [computers or the Internet]. *I have* means *I AM* because you always have what you are and you always do what you are."

6. Faith is the key. Believe you receive! According to your faith, it is done unto you, so hold your faith high. Believe in the process, which is infallible. The Golden Key to success is in BELIEVING YOU RECEIVE! So, Believe! Expect something wonderful to happen! That it is happening now!

Robert Russell wrote, "Jesus was never averse to our praying for things that are in accord with God's purpose. What He insisted upon was the acceptance and belief that we *already have* them in our possession."

7. "With good to all concerned", is a vital part of the Recipe. You want only good to come to you and everyone who has anything to do with your multiplied money. There is no way of knowing who or how many people have something to do with the

multiplied money that comes to you. When you declare this part of the Recipe, you are assuring that anyone who has anything to do with your multiplied money is blessed in some way. Therefore, no harm can come to anyone and you wouldn't want that. This especially applies to yourself because you don't want your multiplied money to come in negative ways that are harmful to you, only in helpful, peaceful and uplifting ways.

8. Love is essential. With all the money you give as seed, give lots of love with it. Give money and use the Recipe lovingly. Love is the fulfilling energy that drives multiplied money to you. It is the real essence of this divinely prospering activity.

9. You are working with the Law of Attraction (Giving and Receiving). Be enthusiastic, excited and expectant. The Law works as you con-scientiously work with it. It is a golden opportunity to multiply your money and increase your wealth as you bless countless other people in the process.

Do not worry about when you give money at different times and in different amounts. Let's say that you give $5 to someone and a little while later you give $10 to another person, and give several $1 gifts, just make your claim using the Recipe each time. It is not necessary to keep tract unless you want to. Some people do and that's okay. You needn't add up all you have given in a day and make your claim again. The Universe, which is intelligent, thinking Substance, surely knows how to add and multiply and produce your multiplied money for you. And, it is amazingly fast in doing so! It is calculating everything even as you are planting the money seed. Trust the process. Never be concerned with *how* your multiplied money is coming to you, or sit around anxiously looking for it. Just know that it is, already has, and be grateful.

A while after I presented a Seed Money Seminar at the Unity Church in Everett, Washington, I received a letter containing a seed money offering of $100. The writer, a real estate agent said, "Following my contribution of seed money which was $100 then, sales began to flow in at a rate far above average. The interesting thing was that many of the accounts were of the deferred commission kind, which means that money will be coming in over a period of a few years. I feel that this is a definite response to my planting money at your seminar, and from using the Recipe for multiplied money.

"In real estate we often state that it seems to be always feast or famine, but because of recent sales, I will receive a steady income during the winter months when sales tend to slow down. My multiplied money will seem ten times more important to me then!

"I have always believed and affirmed, 'My good comes through me, and not just to me.' Every sale lately has benefited many others, and I have been much more prosperous since I've been working on a shared-commission arrangement rather than just seeking a commission for myself alone. I find that my prosperity adventures are a constant source of excitement and delight in the proven love of my Father-God."

"Not long after that, she wrote again to say, "More good news! Right after my first letter to you, we made a really good sale, and I believe my share of it is further return on my seed money. My prosperity cup runs over!"

This is exactly what happens when you use money as seed. Your prosperity cup overflows! I have received many letters from this person telling me of the great demonstrations of multiplied money by working in harmony with the principle.

A person, who worked in mutual funds, told me, "Since attending your Seminar, where I gave a seed money offering of $250, I did $25,000 worth of business plus a promise of $12,000 more. This gives me a real nice commission."

A short time later, this person wrote again to say, "I just received a substantial check I wasn't expecting, from a commission on a stock sale." This person secretly planted money as seed, made her tenfold claim and it worked beautifully for her.

Here are some things for you to do to help you use money as seed and successfully reap a harvest of multiplied money:

1. Give your money to any individual, church, ministry, organization or institution for any good purpose.

2. Your tithe should *not* be used as seed money. The tithe should always be given to God's work through your church, ministry, spiritual organization, or person who feeds you spiritually.

3. Seed money is given in addition to your tithe.

9

Important Points for Multiplying Your Money

Never pass up an opportunity to give Seed Money and make your tenfold claim on The Infinite. Opportunities are as numerous as there are people! Look for opportunities and they will appear; in fact, when you are focused on giving money, the opportunities will find you!

Keep money in various denominations handy for the purpose of "planting" it as seed. When you do plant it, make your claim using the proven recipe for multiplying your money. No one needs to know what you are doing. It is better to keep quiet and let others become aware of your increasing prosperity. Then, you can tell them! Give them a copy of this book!

Give any amount of money: $1, $5, $10, $50, $100, $1,000, and more. When you begin to realize the power of planting money, making your tenfold claim, and that it works, you will never want to stop! If using money as seed for the purpose of multiplying your money is new to you, you might want to start rather small, whatever you can comfortably do. But don't be too comfortable! It is good to stretch! As you progress, you can always increase the amounts you give, and this will occur naturally as you persist.

When an opportunity for you to give arises rather unexpectedly, you can do one of two things: (1) You can refuse to give, ignore the opportunity and miss out on claiming and receiving a tenfold return and the joy of receiving multiplied money, or, (2) Graciously and promptly accept the opportunity with great gratitude, make your tenfold claim and joyously and enthusiastically expect your money to multiply, as though it already has! I believe you know which choice to make.

In giving money as seed, simply multiply the amount by ten, in your mind. For instance, if you give $5.00, that will be $50.00 in multiplied money. For $100, that will compute to $1000.00 in multiplied money. For $1,000 planted, your multiplied money return is $10,000. For $5,000 planted, your return is $50,000 in multiplied money! The principle is the same for all amounts of money you give as seed.

When you do something for someone but are not paid for doing that, it is perfectly legitimate for you to make your tenfold claim for multiplied money on the value of what you do. Simply calculate the value of it. This includes any kind of service or volunteer work. While it is a good thing to be of as much help as possible, that is, to volunteer for worthy projects, for which you do not expect to be paid, it is perfectly okay for you to calculate the value of your time and effort and make your tenfold claim. You don't need to make a big thing of this, just simply calculate, evaluate and gratefully make your claim. If more people knew this secret, and practiced it, more people would volunteer!

If you take a friend, business associate, or client to lunch and you pay for their lunch, be sure to make your tenfold claim on the price of their lunch. And, don't forget to do the same on the tip! A tip is a gift and a wonderful opportunity for you to give and make your tenfold claim and reap more multiplied money. Do the same whenever and wherever you tip someone such as taxi drivers, barbers, massage therapists, hotel personnel, waiters/waitresses, and many others whose income is largely derived from tips. If you receive help from a minister or other counselor who does not make a specific charge, and you give them an offering, remember to make your tenfold claim.

If you give financially to the Red Cross, Salvation Army, Goodwill, Habitat for Humanity, The Nature Conservancy, or any other agency that depends on voluntary giving, you have every right to give money as seed and make your tenfold claim on it. There is absolutely nothing wrong in doing this. In fact, it is a wise thing to do because it keeps all lack out of your mind, you feel better when you do, and it is a wonderful opportunity to give and multiply your money while helping others. As your money multiplies, you have more to give away and more for your own good use.

Birthday gifts, anniversary gifts, Christmas gifts, other holiday gifts, special occasion gifts, Thank You gifts, no reason gifts, just to be nice gifts, graduation gifts, all kinds of gifts are opportunities to make your tenfold claim for multiplied money.

When you think about it, this activity is really more about giving than receiving, but the way the Universe works It just can't help but give you ten times what you give when you make your claim using the Recipe for Multiplied Money.

When you give money as seed, and make your tenfold claim, expect money, or its equivalent, to come to you in whatever manner and form it wants to. The rule is: When you gift another person with money, and make your tenfold claim, the Universe is going to gift you with ten times that amount, or more. It may not always come in the form of money. So accept your reward in whatever way the Universe wants to bless you.

With this in mind, if someone gives you something of value, but you don't like it, accept it graciously. You can sell it, or give it to someone else and make your tenfold claim on its value.

10

Daily Declarations of Truth

*Speak these Truths every day
with your practice of Multiplied Money.*

*I AM the Administrator of Universal Substance,
which is always permeating everything including my
mind, body and life.*

*I AM the Director of Universal Substance, which
knows only to do what I direct it to do.*

*All of my thoughts, mental images, words and
feelings form this intelligent Substance into the
conditions and circumstances of my life and
environment.*

*None of my thoughts, mental images, words or
feelings ever return to me void, therefore, I am
always mindful that my thoughts, mental images,
words and feelings are positive, uplifting, loving and*

prospering in every way, and in harmony with the universal Laws of Attraction and Giving and Receiving.

By my thought and action, I am richly blessed with Peace of Mind, Life, Love, Happiness, Harmony, Wisdom, Health, and Financial Abundance.

I lovingly and freely share my wealth with other people as gifts of money and service in every positive way, and declare my tenfold return on all of these from Universal Substance. The Universe positively gives me my tenfold return and my money multiplies in amazing ways NOW.

In perfect Faith, I believe I receive! I BELIEVE I HAVE ALREADY RECEIVED! Every day, with practice and persistence, my capacity to receive continually increases, expands and magnifies, and my Money Multiplies!

Every day, in every way, I am growing richer and richer. Through my daily practice of planting seeds of money, I reap a harvest of Multiplied Money. My wealth constantly increases, and my joy overflows. Thank You, God, I am grateful!

11

The Gratitude Attitude

Gratitude is an integral part of the Law of Tenfold Return. Gratitude opens, and keeps open, the doors of abundance. It quickens your return and brings it to you more easily. As you give money and use the Recipe, it is important to sincerely give thanks for your tenfold return just as though you have already received it. With that attitude you give from a consciousness of *having*, rather than of lack.

Direct your thanks toward the Source when you say, *"Thank You! Thank You! Thank You!"* By giving thanks for what you already have, including that which you are giving as seed, you expand it to its full tenfold return, and more. Gratitude is a powerful magnet. That's because it is love expressed. Speaking of love, remember that love is the most important thing in the world. Let your practice of multiplying your money be done in love and it will be a marvelous experience for you and the countless other people you will bless.

Three Essentials to Success & Prosperity

1. You must know that Substance is that from which everything comes.

2. You must know that Substance *always* fulfills your desires according to the claims you make upon it.

3. You must consciously relate and resonate with Substance through heartfelt gratitude.

Many people fail to prosper because of a lack of gratitude. Try as they may to prosper, unless they have a deep sense of gratitude and freely express it, they will not truly prosper. It is true that people can accumulate a lot of money without being grateful, and some do. But getting money that way lacks the essential ingredients of love, joy and creativity and is therefore cold and not lasting.

I talked with a lady a few times who had asked me to pray with her for prosperity. Weeks and months went by with nothing of any consequence happening. Why she didn't prosper puzzled me until one day, while talking with her by phone, I realized that she had a bitter and complaining attitude toward life. When I talked with her about this and suggested she practice being grateful, she said she had nothing to be grateful for. I didn't believe her and kept on until I eventually convinced her to start making a gratitude list. Grudgingly, at first, she did and then she was amazed at how many things she wrote on her list, and it grew daily. Before long, she excitedly told me that for some unknown reason, her financial income had improved and her health and happiness were better, too. I told her that this always happens when one develops a gratitude attitude. It never fails.

Gratitude is Love in expression. Gratitude causes you to live close to God, the Source. The more grateful you are toward God, the easier and faster it is for you to prosper, and greater is your supply. You are healthier and happier, too.

Gratitude helps you to stay focused on God, buoys your faith, keeps you optimistic and protects you from believing that your supply can be limited. If you truly desire to prosper, you will willingly and completely cooperate with the Law of Gratitude.

When your mind is filled with praise and thanksgiving toward the Source, it is giving expression to the powerful force of Love. You are not only prevented from failing, you are pushed forward toward your desired good. By being grateful, you unleash powerful magnetic energy that unerringly draws you and your desired good together. Gratitude is working in full cooperation with the Law of Attraction.

The closer you are to God, in consciousness, the better, and nothing is more powerful for successful accomplishment than gratitude.

You do not really need anything to be grateful for – just be grateful! When your heart is filled with gratitude, your life is filled with beautiful experiences. To God, it really doesn't matter and doesn't influence Him one way or another. God is never whimsical, meaning that He changes is Mind, or acts in certain ways toward some people and differently toward others. Some people may believe this, but it is not true. If it were true, then God could not be God. God never changes. His infinite love flows constantly and perfectly. That is why God, as Love, is the fulfilling Substance continually providing for you.

God only knows to love and provide for you whether or not you are grateful. Why, then, should you be grateful? Because, as I have tried to make clear, gratitude creates a free and open channel (your mind) through which Substance flows more easily and copiously. It is safe to say that gratitude is an extremely profitable practice!

A lady in North Dakota wrote to me to say that until she learned to be genuinely grateful, her level of prosperity was very low. She said that when she expressed gratitude, it was rather shallow without much feeling. Being truly grateful was difficult for her at first, but as she persisted, things began to change, mostly within her. Then, one day quite unexpectedly, she was informed that she was receiving a substantial raise in pay at her company. As it turned out, the boss was very happy with her improved attitude and the pleasant way she interacted with other employees. As this lady continued to raise her level of real gratitude, her prosperity level raised in delightful ways, too.

As I have said, it is not necessary to thank God for things, even the great good God pours out for you. Some people have said that we should thank God for everything, even our troubles and challenges. While it is beneficial to be grateful for the good you receive, never thank God for troubles or challenges. God didn't give them to you! You created them yourself through your own wrong thinking, or disobedience to divine law. Problems and challenges are often "growth curves." They will not keep you down unless you dwell on them and would rather stay down. Give thanks for the growth they have caused you to make.

Do not waste time and energy beating up on yourself. Forgive yourself, quickly and completely, taking the lesson from that experience and move forward. Be grateful that you have learned your lesson and gained something valuable. Be thankful for the wisdom God has given you to correct mistakes, profit by them, and to grow in your understanding of His infinite love and all-provision for you.

When things are tough, that is the time for a greater expression of gratitude, not for "hard times," but just for the sake of being grateful. Be thankful that you live in a Universe of infinite plenty – plenty of love, all you could ever need. And, all of the life, peace, Substance, wisdom, power, energy there is. It's all yours!

Thanksgiving keeps your consciousness centered in, and unified with Substance. That is why a gratitude attitude is so important. It is out of omnipresent Substance that all the good you desire, comes. The more deeply you are connected to Substance, the greater is your happiness, success, peace of mind, and all-around well being.

While being thankful for *exterior* things is of great value, being thankful for *interior* things is of far greater value. If you truly desire to improve your prosperity level, improve your gratitude level.

Gratitude lifts your vision and clears your mind. Gratitude frees the creative juices within. It opens the way for prospering ideas to flow.

Gratitude – a truly thank-full heart – is your Golden Key to riches!

Read more about Gratitude in the author's book, *How to Have 'Unexpected' Income.*

12

Mystic Nourishment

Dr. Emma Smiley wrote in *Bread Of Life*, "Mystic Nourishment is obtained from every word, from every feeling and act that adds to our joy of living, that heals our bodies and frees us from fear. Men may learn the joy of living and be mystically nourished through tithing."

When you buy food from a market and consume it, you realize whether or not it is of value by the nourishment the food gives your body.

There is only one way to prove to yourself the value of anything and that is through using it. If something you do adds to your enjoyment of life, then it is of value to you, and to humanity. If it lessens life, then it has no real value.

Emma Smiley believed that tithing is the answer to spiritually feeding the world. Sure, there is plenty of religiosity, but that has never solved anything in the world and has often added to the lack of peace, life, and abundance. Spirituality is what the world needs and it comes through people learning and becoming attuned to God. Tithing has a mystical quality that is required.

You do not buy food for your body in order to prosper, but to make it strong and healthy, and to give it energy so you may accomplish things that are important to you. By the same token, you do not tithe so that you may prosper, but to feed and nourish your consciousness. You do so because you know it makes you aware of the Presence of God. Emma Smiley further states, "So you may better know the great truth on which all true prosperity is based: God is Adequate to provide all that you need, whether little or much."

Dissolve in your belief system that poverty is God's will. It is not! It has never been true and never can be true. There is nothing spiritual about being poor. God did not, could not put you or any of His children here without adequately providing for each and every one. When you know that God is all there is, then you know that God is everywhere, all the time. God is the very substance of your body and the invisible substance of your mind, and the very air you breathe.

Therefore, it should be easy for you to choose to believe in abundant provision rather than lack of supply. You must choose one or the other. Since God has always been more than adequate in your life, regardless of your awareness, then God is more than adequate now. The good news is that God is *always sufficient,* and then some! If this weren't true, then God wouldn't be God.

If you are thinking of tithing, it would be wise for you to ask if you believe God to be wholly able to provide for you. If you do not believe He is, it doesn't mean there is something wrong with the principle of tithing, but with your perception of God, especially as a wise, loving and most beneficent provider. Change your concept of God and you will be amazed at the change in your consciousness, and subsequently in your life and affairs.

Oftentimes, a person will hesitate to tithe because he or she has not yet gained the understanding and realization that God is only Good, the only Power and Presence. Work on gaining the correct perception of God and you will have sufficient reason to no longer hesitate to tithe.

You should understand that God does not punish anyone who does not tithe. Sometimes, it may seem that way, but when you know God as Infinite Love, then you know that God does not punish because God *cannot* punish.

What happens, then, when a person refrains from tithing and suffers lack? It is not that God is punishing him or her for not tithing, but because he or she is not cooperating with the law of giving and receiving. Often this is caused by fear or a deep sense of lack. Actually, when that happens, it is a conscious or unconscious separation from God; a feeling of being disconnected from the Source. That is nothing that God does but what one does to oneself. When you flick a light switch to turn off electricity, the electricity doesn't punish you; by your action you interrupted the flow. If a person decided to eat food that was not good for him and became ill, it wasn't something that God did to him, but something he chose for himself.

Tithing is one of the best ways to connect with the Source. It makes the divine connection between God and your finances through your consciousness. Tithing is not just working with the law of giving and receiving; it is proving that you really do believe that God is more than sufficient to provide for you.

The secret of demonstrating prosperity

The secret of demonstrating prosperity in a spiritual way – and on no other basis can your prosperity ever be secure – is to understand and to know to the point of realization, that the one and only Source of your supply is God. Your business, employment, investments, clients, and customers are channels through which God's rich supply comes to you moment by moment.

When you tithe with this understanding, which is spiritual, it is truly the hard evidence that you have accepted this position. And the consequences of that acceptance are rich abundance – prosperity at its best.

It should be easier, now, to see the difference between the spiritual practice of tithing rather than doing so mechanically. When you tithe as an expression of spiritual understanding, it is a sure-fire success. If you tithe as a selfish investment, you can count on failure. In the latter, you'd be better off to hang on to the money because you will probably need it. You may have a greater belief in lack than in abundance. When you tithe in faith, you know it is the right thing to do. You are paying for your spiritual nourishment and you may be assured that not only will all your needs be met, but there will always be plenty of money!

I want to reiterate an important aspect of tithing so as to eliminate any confusion about it. Tithing does not include charity or material giving. Tithing is devoted to helping to spread Truth around our planet. This is done by financially supporting the activities, people, and institutions that are actually engaged in this important spiritual work.

When you understand this Spiritual idea, you are keenly aware that the one and only thing that the world needs to be free from its difficulties is the knowledge of spiritual Truth. Until an individual comes to this realization, no other thing will bring benefit to him; no amount of secular learning, scientific breakthrough, no social reform schemes, no political doctoring, can ever do any authentic good. Once this knowledge does become widely known, all political and social difficulties will automatically be adjusted, charities will no longer be needed. It is good to give money toward good works, but give money as seed (not your tithe) and claim your tenfold return. Your first duty, of course, is to use your tithe toward the spreading of spiritual Truth.

The settling of the matter of the tithe is very simple. As some may have erroneously believed, it doesn't mean a tenth of the amount one is able to save from his income for say, a month. It means a tenth of one's whole income. If you are in business, you tithe on the net profit. However, the tithe must be given *before* personal or living expenses are deducted. Those who receive a salary, certain deductions are usually made; however, the tithe is figured on the gross salary *before* deductions. The same is true with money received from investments such as stocks and bonds.

It should be understood that there is no obligation for anyone to tithe until he arrives at the state of consciousness when tithing is his choice. Actually, it is better that he not start to tithe until he is ready to do so. Tithing should never be done grudgingly or with misgivings out of a sense of duty. That is fear. Prosperity is not produced from fear.

The fact is that tithing is an exceptionally efficient act of Faith. Often it happens that a Truth student will whole-heartedly put his trust wholly in God. This is understanding faith. When you whole-heartedly desire, you have it, although at first, you may not have a sense of solid conviction. You might even think of yourself as having a lack of faith when in reality, that isn't true.

When you practice tithing as a result of honestly knowing that it is the right thing to do, this will be the proof of your faith, regardless of the feelings you might have at the moment.

Sometimes, when a person is experiencing financial pressure from not having enough money, he may think it is impossible for him to tithe at that time, so he thinks it is okay to put it off until circumstances improve. This is erroneous thinking. In truth, the greater the present financial need, the greater is the need to tithe. The present difficulty is always due to one's mental attitude that may be subconscious, and his circumstances can't improve until he has made a correction in this. Then he tithes in faith, love and gratitude.

When you truly tithe, you may be sure that it will be followed by the demonstration of financial and other improvements.

Since tithing is the giving of ten percent of your income, the less your income, the less your tithe; the larger your income, the larger is your tithe. There is an automatic adjustment as your income grows.

How often should you tithe? The answer is quite simple. The right time to tithe is upon receiving financial income, whether it is daily, weekly, monthly, and at other times. You are wise to give smaller tithes more often than holding on to the money until you can give larger amounts. It is a good idea to pray for guidance concerning this, and then follow that guidance.

Understand that since you are an integral part of God, when you give God His ten percent, through His channels of spiritual instruction, you ultimately give to yourself. This is true because through the giving of your tenth, you are helping those channels to provide you with your spiritual groceries.

John Murray wrote: "Those who tithe are always certain that they have God for a partner." In other words, through tithing you create a divine partnership that knows only how to prosper. It is a win-win situation in every sense of the word.

Bring all of the tithes – the whole tenth of your income – into the storehouse, that there may be food in My house, and prove Me now by it, says the Lord of hosts, if I will not open the windows of heaven for you and pour you out a blessing that there shall not be room enough to receive it. – *Malachi 3:10* (Amplified Old Testament)

A man who began tithing years ago soon saw his income start to grow. He no longer worried about money and he did not experience financial strain or pain, or undesirable surprises. Instead, since starting to tithe, his financial surprises were all good ones.

Tithing caused money to come to him seemingly from "out of the blue." Of course it came because of his working with the law. In addition, he was surprised at how much further his money went. He said that tithing seems to have a rubberizing effect in that it somehow causes money to stretch.

Giving a tenth of your whole income to God's good work opens the way for rich financial increase and protects you from negative experiences. Tithing makes a "divine connection" between you, your finances, and the Source of all wealth. It is one of the surest ways I know to verify within your consciousness that God is the Source of your supply, and to establish a link with the supply itself.

Another good thing about tithing is that it helps to eliminate those negative financial surprises that no one really needs. Those surprises sometimes come in the form of car repairs, doctor and hospital bills, lawsuits, and other things that require money that you would rather use for something more enjoyable.

The more you consciously connect with the Source, the easier life is, with less worry about financial matters. Because you know where your supply is – within yourself and everywhere present – you don't have to look very far, because *It is always where you are!*

Tithing helps you to open your mind to rich ideas. Many people have been exceedingly prospered through the tithing practice. For example, LeTourneau was given the idea for the huge earth-moving machines from which he became a multi-millionaire. Many exceptionally wealthy people attribute their financial success to tithing.

When you tithe, you prosper because it creates abundance in consciousness, which naturally out-pictures as greater prosperity in your life.

13

Questions & Answers About Tithing

*From a mystical standpoint
tithing is a consciousness of God first.*
-- Jim Rosemergy, *Even Mystics Have Bills to Pay*

What is a tithe?

A tithe is ten percent of your whole income, before deductions. It is not 1% or 5%, but 10%. Some metaphysical teachers may tell you that it is okay to start out with only 1% or maybe 5% and build up to the full 10%; however, tithe means tenth. It is nothing less than 10%. If you were to give less than the whole 10%, you are not tithing. It would indicate that you have more work to do in consciously connecting with the Source and in accepting that you live in an over-abundant Universe, which knows only to provide for you. It also implies that you have some fear to release along with some no-longer working, very limiting beliefs. Those who are serious about raising their level of prosperity, and have a real desire for the law of increase to work fully for them, boldly give the full 10% at the beginning and continue doing so. You are wise to make a decision to change your financial status and persistently follow up with positive action.

If you want the Universe to give full measure to you, you must give in the same way. You cannot afford to fool around with less than the full 10%. You do not want only a portion of the riches that the Source has for you; you want it all! Do your part and God will never fail to do His.

I know from my own experience how difficult it can be to start giving 10% of all you receive back to God, if you are not accustomed to doing so. I struggled with it for quite a while until I realized that I had to do something because I was wallowing in more lack than I really desired. So, I made a decision to give the full 10% in order to put the tithing principle to the test. To my amazement, it worked! I slowly began to prosper as old fears and negative beliefs began dropping away. I was much happier, too.

If you truly desire to take a positive prospering step toward eliminating financial lack, then take the plunge. Start with 10% and keep at it faithfully. You will have taken a big step toward financial abundance. Do it with love and joy and you will win!

A tithe is not a gift, nor is it charity. Neither is it a reward or payment for services. Do not use your tithe to pay bills or to help relatives and friends. When you want to help others, financially, give them Seed Money and claim your tenfold return as explained in Chapter 7 of this book. Make sure you use your tithe for nothing but to further God's Truth on Mother Earth.

In other words, give back to God 10% and use the rest for other things. Take it right off the top and give it *first* before using the money for something else. When you make a habit of giving to God first, you'll be surprised at how far your money goes!

If you think you cannot afford to tithe and must use the money for personal things, you do not yet understand the Law of Increase or the Law of Giving and Receiving. Seek for more under- standing until it becomes clear to you that giving a full ten percent back to the Source is the surest and most practical way of establishing yourself in constant financial plenty. You will have then created within you, the consciousness that God is adequate to provide for you.

The tithe is money dedicated to God's work on Mother Earth and it is incorrect to use it for any- thing except to further His work.

Do not wait until you fully understand the Law of Increase. Put your faith into what you do and trust the Universe to respond to the faith you put in It. It may surprise you – especially when you give in love and joy.

Where should you give your tithe?

Give your tithe to a church or spiritual organization, minister, or other person who is directly involved in spiritual work. It is best to give where you are receiving your spiritual food. Do not continue to give financially to a church or spiritual organization with which you are no longer involved, or is not spiritually feeding you. Support those who are feeding you spiritually, especially those from whom you learn the dynamic laws and principles that spiritually feed you and help to increase your prosperity. In so doing, you place yourself in direct relation to the Source.

Would you like to have a rich relative who can really support you? God, your Father-God, and Source of all your good, is the richest relative you could ever have! His resources are limitless and are yours for the asking, appropriating and receiving when you act in harmony with His laws and principles.

Where you give your tithe is of utmost importance. While it is okay to spread your tithe around, it is good to make your tithe checks, or electronic tithes, as large as possible, and to make your main channel of spiritual food as financially sound as possible.

What are the results of tithing?

One of the unexpected benefits of tithing is that it gives you divine protection, shielding you from many of the negative aspects of life. It gives you the wisdom to use your money more wisely. When I have found it necessary to really look to God for increase, I know, because of being a long-standing tither, that everything will be taken care of. I know that I am divinely protected so there is nothing to fear. Thus, I relax, let go, and let God take care of things, which He *always* does. It really helps to know that God is adequate, whatever the need or desire. This significantly adds to your peace of mind.

You should expect to experience an increase in financial and other forms of prosperity. One of the reasons for that is because through tithing, you establish a divine partnership with God, the Source, your Senior Partner. His resources are infinite! This connectedness has an accumulative, multiplying effect.

You simply cannot out-give God! Try your best, but it can't be done. You cannot ask for a better "financial connection," which is more correctly a spiritual connection with the Source of all your good. God never fails; He never has and never will. If you are not already doing so, the best way to prove this is to begin tithing now and continue doing so.

A businesswoman made an agreement with God when she opened a new store. She agreed to give back to God 10% of all she received, right off the top. From the beginning, her new business flourished, becoming more prosperous than she had thought possible.

A chiropractor and his wife learned the value of tithing and made a covenant to give at least 10% back to God. They did this from the beginning. Sometimes it was a bit of a struggle getting their new practice going, but when I reminded them that since they were tithers, their success and prosperity were assured. They have continued to persist in faith and their practice prospered as they served more and more people.

A lady in Illinois wrote to tell me that after about a week of using the following affirmation, *Tithing from my whole income, I am now prospered, and my life is happy and complete,* she and her husband received a three-week vacation to California, all expenses paid. They stayed in the best hotel near the beach and had a wonderful time!

She said, "We were both unemployed and hadn't tithed for about two months when we decided to start again. I sent my tithe and continued to declare that God is truly the Source of our supply and would provide His own amazing channels for our prosperity.

"The day I sent the tithe, my husband heard of a good paying job and two days later he got it. I will be starting back to work soon, too. Thanks for helping us realize the importance of giving our tenth to God, first. We have learned a valuable lesson, and will continue to tithe. It surely does work!"

Another important result of tithing is better health, which naturally follows from being set free from worry over a lack of money, or people stealing from you. Money worries are a primary cause of ill health. They can cause fear, frustration, loss of sleep, anxiety and resentment. Tithing empowers you and gives you peace and freedom.

Still another effect of tithing is the joy and happiness that comes through having an intimate relationship with the Source. It enables you to relax and go about your daily activities confidently knowing that everything is provided for. Whatever the need, God provides.

A person in California wrote to say, "Sometimes in our busy schedules and trying to make ends meet, we forget about the opportunity to increase our abundance. It had been quite a while since I had given my tithe when I was presented with the opportunity at two Christmas candle lighting services. A few days later, I received an unexpected Christmas bonus from one of my employers. Here is my grateful tithe from this 'unexpected' income."

Someone in Ohio wrote: "Not only was I able to take a really super vacation, I've been offered a new job that pays over $4,000 per year more than the one I had just lost. I am so thankful that I have kept on tithing and using the *Prayer Treatment for 'Unexpected' Income. Together they have worked financial miracles in my life! I have a new attitude of positive expectancy."

*The Prayer-Treatment for 'Unexpected' Income is found in the author's book, How To Have 'Unexpected' Income. Look for this great prosperity book in Unity or Religious Science book stores, or order directly from the author.

Those who are truly prosperous know the value of "ten" in relation to prosperity. "Ten" is the magic number of increase used successfully by prosperous people of ancient times as well as modern times. People who prosper accept without question, the value of voluntarily tithing ten percent of their whole income to God's work where they are learning the prospering Truth.

Does tithing really work?

Yes. It is has always worked for those who practice faithfully in the right attitude. To be most effective, tithing should be practiced *voluntarily* through understanding of the law of giving and receiving, and in faith and joy. While it may be easier for a person to tithe when *required* to, it is better to do it *lovingly* and *freely* without coercion.

Every phase of your life becomes better, more harmonious, and filled with right conditions and experiences when you faithfully tithe. That is because you are cooperating with one of the oldest and most beneficial prosperity laws, that of gratitude. Your gratitude attitude not only opens prosperity doors, but keeps them open. Tithing is a practical way of saying, "Thank You, God, for Your abundant provision for me." It is wise, therefore, to give your tithe lovingly and gratefully, as well as consistently. While a lot of thought should be put into tithing, it is always best when it comes from a grateful heart! Consider the following from a tither in Montana:

"I am so grateful I began the practice of tithing many years ago. At first, I was very mechanical about tithing my income to the church I attended, but I had a sense of peace from the start. Then, I took Stretton Smith's 4-T Prosperity class. Afterward, I also tithed my time and talent to the church I was attending at that time.

"What I have come to understand is that tithing is simply *gratitude*. Giving back to the Source of Abundance is surely an opportunity to say 'Thank You' to the God-Presence for the blessings which flow to me through the many individualizations of God with whom I interact. The joy and blessings which return to me increase the joy in my life as well as a sense of belonging to the Universe; of being a part of the reciprocal giving and receiving in constant flow. What I give makes a difference. We've all been instructed that one must give in order to receive. However, it does no good to give out a sense of obligation. Love, genuine appreciation, and enthusiasm for increase of the joy we have received, must be the deciding factors.

"Tithing is essential in order to experience the fullness of the life we have come here to enjoy. The more gratitude we express, the more joy we experience." – Jana Ostrom in Montana

A woman in Michigan said that things improved dramatically in her home when she began to tithe. She wrote: "Since I have been tithing at least ten percent of my income, I have seen a wonderful change of attitude in my home. Everyone in my family, as well as my coworkers, seems to be more positive. We have been able to pay off a lot of bills, and I've been getting 'A's and 'B's at school. I feel more self confident and sure of myself. Continually, I remind myself that God is my source and there are no limitations in my mind, body, or financial affairs. I attribute all this to tithing which surely helps me be more consciously connected to God. Tithing is certainly working for me!"

When you tithe, does it always bring immediate increase?

Tithers usually discover that they begin to prosper financially when they invoke the prosperity law of tithing. Often, when there are no immediate outward rewards from tithing, it is never because of the tithing law, but because a person probably has some rather strong lack or fear issues that need to be cleared up. Sometimes anger and resentment toward someone, or even a distrust of God, will cause delay, or stop the flow of divine substance, completely.

Often increase comes rather quickly, although tithing, in its truest sense, is not done to bring financial increase, but to prove God's adequacy. It is done to give evidence to your acceptance of the Truth that God is adequate to provide for you, "according to His riches." His riches, of course, are infinite. Your tithe is payment for your spiritual food.

When you tithe in this realization, you have a consciousness of the presence of God, which is your true prosperity. This always leads to more peace, love, health and happiness and greater financial supply.

You can be sure that when you begin to tithe, you will prosper more. More money is a natural outworking of the Law of Increase faithfully applied. Even if it seems to take longer than you think it should, the "gold dust" is gathering for you and will begin to settle upon you soon!

If your desired financial abundance seems slow in coming, or there are some financial challenges, these will not be a problem to you because you are a tither and you have the inner assurance that all is well. You need only be patient and hold to your faith in God to provide for you. You know your greater good is on its way to you now.

I do not mean to imply that because you are a tither, you will never have financial challenges. If they do come, because of your direct connection with the Source, which you create by tithing, you need only to persist in faith assured that everything is really okay. You *know* it is!

Faithful tithers know they have a divine connection with God, the Source. They know they are always divinely protected, and even if some doors appear to be closed, or if there are challenges, things will work out. They know they will be better off than before. Their prosperity is assured.

When you tithe, and there appear to be delays or financial challenges, check up on your attitude. Are you still coming from fear? Fear is like a kink in the hose. Release the fear and come only from love. Let go of old, stingy, grasping attitudes of mind, especially where it concerns money. Know that as a child of God you are entitled to the riches of the Kingdom.

As you release fear, let go of every concept or belief in lack or limitation. Expand your realization of God's loving, all-providing Substance. Then tithe from this consciousness. I believe things will open up for you rather quickly. Tithing, like all spiritual Laws and Principles, must be done in the right attitude, faith, love and gratitude. It is truly a spiritual activity. You merely use money in the process and God gives the increase!

What is the genuine purpose and law of tithing?

The answer to this question is found in Malachi 3:10. *Bring the full tithes into the store-house, that there may be food in my house; and thereby put me to the test, says the Lord of hosts, if I will not open the windows of heaven for you and pour down for you an overflowing blessing.* (Revised Standard Version)

The purpose of tithing:

The first purpose of tithing is to prove you believe God is adequate to provide for you. Secondly, is the support of individuals or organizations engaged in Spiritual activity where the knowledge and power of God is promoted. Specifically, it is the support of those from whom you receive your spiritual food in order to prosper in every area of life.

The law of tithing:

The law of tithing is the Law of Giving and Receiving. Through this a definite connection is created between cause and effect, which is innately supported and is permanent in nature. If a break in the process happens, there is a corresponding diminishing in the flow of Substance. This is exemplified by the story of the Prodigal Son. He separated his inheritance from his father and soon came to want. The Law amplifies and perpetuates that which it acts upon. The Prodigal Son's separation from his father is a mental separation. It is a conscious disconnect from the Source. Many people suffer the same thing and "come to want" like the Prodigal Son. When you consciously return to the Father, the inner spiritual connection is restored and you are prospered. The Father is pure Love and loves to throw parties for His children.

Through tithing, the connection is secure and cannot be broken. There is no separation from the source of your wealth. It keeps your financial, and all your affairs, in constant contact with the Source and Its creative power. The results of tithing are dependent upon faithful observance of the Law.

To whom is the tithe given?

As in ancient times, the tithe is given where you are in direct contact with spiritual work. This does not necessarily mean the largest spiritual organization, but that particular individual or organization or predominate source where you are receiving clear spiritual help or inspiration. To give to the least of these is to give to the whole. Only through the continuance of these spiritual individuals, organizations, and movements, are the greatest ideals preserved. By supporting these with your tithes, you are actually supporting yourself.

A spiritual ministry can be no stronger than the support its followers allow it to be. Spiritual workers and students of spiritual things are wise when they see to it that their channels of spiritual food are well supported.

To safeguard your own best interests, you are wise to make your channel or channels of spiritual food (enlightenment) just as strong as you possibly can. You are also wise to do all you can in thought, word, and act to perfect those channels you look to for spiritual sustenance. When a spiritual individual or organization is free from financial strain, they are much more empowered to provide you with spiritual enlightenment to help you grow spiritually.

A spiritual ministry, which is starving financially, cannot give to you or to others, the best in spiritual food and support. When you see to it that there is "food in my house," the "house" will be in the very best position to serve you and others. Some people have the mistaken belief that ministers and other spiritual counselors work for nothing. This is false. They have bills to pay, too. When you seek their help, pay them generously. They have earned it. If they do not charge a specific fee, give them a portion of your tithe. If you give them money as seed, make your tenfold claim using the Recipe for Multiplied Money.

How is tithing practiced and what are the results of tithing?

Tithing in its truest sense is the setting aside one-tenth, or more, of your whole income. For myself, I have a separate checking account, which I call my giving account. Into this account I place ten percent of all that comes in, and then write my tithe checks from this account.

Gifts, charities, obligations, upkeep of relatives, and so on, should *never* be included in your tithes. (Use *Seed Money* for these.)

The tithe is not money to be used for anything except for the support and furtherance of God's work on Mother Earth. That 10% is dedicated to the Source. The tithe is one-tenth of your entire income that is set aside and used to maintain the divine connection between the Source and your income, or finances.

It is wise to give your tithe as soon and as directly as possible, remembering to do so joyously and lovingly. In your giving, you are simply paying for your Mystic Nourishment.

Tithing is done to preserve an unbroken and always-enlarging contact with the Law of Life. In turn this is made permanent in your affairs and throughout the world.

When you tithe directly to where you receive your present Spiritual food, you have placed yourself in the best direct position with the Law of Giving and Receiving and you are assured of the most direct, abundant and personal rewards. Only by preserving your inner contact with the Law of Life are you in line to receive these blessings. The blessings are a many-fold increase and are not too much for you to expect when you comply with the spirit of the Law.

Since you may have reaped the unwanted results of disobedience to Spiritual Law, it stands to reason that through strict adherence to the Law, your blessings will overflow so that they are more than you can possibly use.

But, of course, the highest and most satisfying reward is the inner realization that you are in harmony with your Real Self. Inner peace is more to be desired than the attainment of outer or material rewards. The sense that you are right brings the most wonderful peace and satisfaction that Life could ever give you. Such inner states must be out-pictured. It is the natural working of the Law of Cause and Effect, or Sowing and Reaping.

Tithing works equally well for individuals and organizations engaged in Spiritual Ministry. They must allow themselves to be guided by Spirit, of course. The same Law is applicable to everyone regardless of what work they are engaged in. It has been said that a church full of tithers is never in debt. This means not only those who attend the church, but also those who work and teach there, and the church itself. Anyone who is engaged in Spiritual work is wise to tithe.

To whom is the tithe paid?

In Old Testament times, the tithe went to the support of the Levites (meaning those who adhere) as adherents of the Spiritual Law. They in turn passed on one tenth of their supply to support the priest. In this way, the structure for perpetuating spiritual ideals was well supported.

One would naturally tithe at the point, or points, where he is in direct contact with spiritual work. This is not necessarily the biggest spiritual organization, but the appropriate individual or organization or source of inspiration. In other words, where a person receives his spiritual enlightenment. These are all stations in the great scheme of spiritual provision. To serve the least of these is to serve the whole. It is only through these spiritual avenues that the greatest ideals have been preserved and they are worthy of genuine cooperation.

Some people may ask, "Shouldn't spiritual work and workers demonstrate their own supply directly?" The answer to this question is "yes." However, God speaks and acts through channels. Therefore, you look to the individual or organization as a channel through which you receive spiritual help and ideas that help you live more abundantly.

In turn, it is absolutely within the province of true spiritual practice that you should be a channel through which God supplies the Minister or the Ministry. It is a good arrangement that works both ways.

In order to safeguard your own best interests, it is imperative for you to help make your chosen channel, or channels, of spiritual support as strong as possible. It is essential, then, for you to strive in thought, word, and act, to keep open and clear, the channel or channels, through which you are spiritually fed.

In so doing, you also help to provide for others to receive spiritual help, and you help lift the consciousness of the world. A starved spiritual ministry is not able to give you the best spiritual support. When you make sure there is plenty of food (financial supply) in the place where you are spiritually fed, you are working in your own best interest.

Letters from tithers:

"Tithing has always been a natural part of my life. Growing up with a mother and grandmother who were farmers, I learned early in life, that you save the **best** 10% of seeds for next years crop. This practice ensures that each year's crop would be as good, or better, than last year's crop. Tithing is the natural order of things; one is to give back part of which one has already received. I have always tithed for this reason, and I believe it helps me stay in the natural flow of life. In order to stay conscious, one cannot breathe in forever, one must also breathe out! Tithing is the same thing." – K. F. in California

Another tither wrote: "I believe in tithing because it is the best way to thank God for His benevolence in all areas of our lives. It is also a wonderful way to show God how much we love Him. Tithing is a method that has helped me in many wonderful ways like none other, for various reasons:

1. It has helped me to be open-minded to the goodness of God.

2. It has helped me to expand my consciousness in the opulence that God has in store for me.

3. It has helped me to focus on abundance instead of scarcity.

4. It is a blessing to be an instrument of God's goodness and provision to bless places that from which I receive my spiritual nourishment.

5. The act of putting God first financially has given me wisdom on how to use the 90% of substance left according to God's plan for my life.

6. I have found that when I give, the 90% goes further.

7. I also have found tithing beneficial because it gives me peace of mind by knowing that God is in charge of all my financial transactions and that He makes me prosper in all my endeavors.

8. Tithing is the best way for me to send a message to the Universe that I depend on God for my every need to be met.

9. Tithing helps me to raise my positive expectancy in the happy financial surprises that God is sending my way.

"I want to share with you another positive outcome that God has caused in my life related to my decision to tithe:

"In 2006, God opened the way for me to go back to Columbia where to human sense it appeared impossible for me to go because I was in debt and I know He blessed me that way due to my faithfulness to and consistency in tithing. When I was in my country on vacation, God provided for my every need for the two weeks I was there, and I even had money to spare. God did a miracle because I owed about $500 to my dad, but he forgave the debt, and now I owe him nothing.

"Still another blessing I have received since I began to tithe is that my headphones for my iPod have lasted for over 7 months. When I didn't practice tithing, I used to buy headphones once a month because they got damaged.

"I notice that my loved ones, my belongings and I are protected by God when I put Him first, financially. Tithing helps me to expect the best and receive the best in every area of my life.

"The best part is that giving makes me richer day by day because God is the Source of my supply.

"It is okay for you to use my name. Thank you for your love and wonderful teachings that are blessing me in infinite ways." – Angie Cruz in New York

Tithing is making this person's life go more smoothly. "Being consistently generous has proven to be a blessing in my life. Tithing reminds me that I have something to give. When I am participating in the circulation of Universe Supply, my life seems to go more smoothly. Maybe the discipline of percentage giving just makes me pay more attention to my budget and therefore I stay within it. Or, maybe having the intention to share somehow activates the Law of Attraction so that as I think thoughts of giving the Universe responds by making sure I have more to give. It is fun to support worthwhile causes and the joy of giving attracts good fortune to me. But however it works, it does work. Giving is as much a part of my spiritual life as prayer, meditation, affirmation, and study. Knowing that I live in an abundant Universe, I freely give and Life generously gives back to me. Tithing is a spiritual law that I teach and practice and highly recommend." – Rev. Durrell Watkins, Sunshine Cathedral, Ft. Lauderdale, Florida

Ten reminders about tithing:

1. Tithe means tenth. It is one-tenth of your whole income *before* deductions, and given regularly.

2. The tithe is given to God through the channel or channels you receive your "spiritual groceries." In other words, fed spiritually, i.e. church, minister, spiritual counselor, or other spiritual person or organization.

3. The tithe is given voluntarily. Some religious institutions require their members to tithe to them. It is spiritually incorrect to demand tithes from anyone for any reason.

4. When you tithe, you may expect to be divinely protected and provided for.

5. You tithe to prove God's adequacy.

6. It is incorrect to tithe to a church you no longer attend, or that doesn't feed you spiritually. Find one that does and support it with your tithes.

7. Tithing makes the divine connection between you, God, and your prosperity.

8. The tithe is not to be used to pay bills, for expenses, food, or to help relatives, or other people. Use money as seed to help others. (See Chapter 7.)

9. The tithe is dedicated money to God's work. It is to be used to help further His work on Mother Earth.

10. Tithing is putting God first in your finances. With tithers, there is never a recession. Tithing puts a spiritual foundation under your finances and business transactions, gives you peace of mind and the assurance that you are always provided for. *It works!*

You do not have to tithe. You may starve if you wish. – Emma Smiley

Our present state of health, happiness,
self-expression, prosperity and
our degree of liberty and freedom are
an exact measure of
our present soul growth. We can
express, attract, hold onto, and use,
only as much as we are.
The way to have more is to
be more today. – Stella Terrell Mann

14

Man's True Quest

If we desire to help a suffering world,
we too will suffer.
That which we think and vision, that toward
which we give our attention today,
manifests in our lives tomorrow.
If we joyously give to the world
our realization of God, the world will be blessed
and we ourselves will become more Godlike.
– Emma Smiley

Man's true quest is to know God, which is his good. When you devote attention to actually practicing the presence of God, God's true nature is revealed to you. When this happens you are joyous and carefree. This always results when you gain this knowledge and understanding. Further, you become aware of God's perfect availability, and that He is completely able to take care of every detail of your daily life. That another way of saying, "With God all things are possible."

The answer to the search for God is the understanding of your relationship with Him. The only reason someone may fear God is that they do not know Him. Too often, it is believed that God is a big, mean old man in the sky somewhere, which, when you understand God's true nature of Love, is ridiculous.

If you know God only as a far-off, erratic being who may or may not answer your prayers, then you will certainly not have any feeling of security and you will experience a hungering and a questing that can never be wholly satisfied.

In order for God to be true to His nature, God must be all there is. Therefore, God must be adequate to solve any problem that may arise. And, answer every prayer. The only way to live fearlessly, beautifully and limitlessly is to know God as the only Presence, the only Power – All there is.

This should give you the understanding and faith to know that you can absolutely depend on God to fulfill your dreams; that He is powerfully able to supply you with all the good you could possibly want or dream of having. This knowing allows you to live a joyous, carefree life.

How may you gain this knowledge and understanding? It is by adhering to a certain principle. This principle may be stated thusly:

Anything to which you give your loyal attention will reveal itself to you. All growth and success hinges on this principle.

When you give your loving attention to knowing God, your problems will cease to be. They will die of neglect. As you continue to give God your faithful attention, you will soon become keenly aware that God truly is greater than any seeming problem or difficult situation. You will learn to depend on the Greater instead of the lesser. You will become like that to which you faithfully give your attention.

When you come to know God as abundance, your life will become abundant. As you know God as the very Life of your body, it will respond by being wholly alive. So it is with knowing God as freedom. This is the Truth that releases you from the bondage of limitation, and that sets you free – free to be all that God wants you to be.

God provides everything in abundance, and so
has provided abundance for you.
What is abundance?
Abundance means that you have such an
amount of money in your possession
that you never have to think about
money. That is abundance, and
nothing less, and nothing more than
that can be called abundance.

– Emmet Fox

15

Your Q Power

R Q Asking the Right Questions?

*The ability to ask the right questions
is what I call your Q Power.
Q stands for Question.*

Some people tend to ask disempowering questions seemingly unaware of the great question answering power of the mind, and the Universe. They ask questions such as, "Why am I so sick?" – "Why do I never have enough money?" – "Why am I so unhappy?" Then they wonder why they aren't healthier, wealthier and happier. Even the latter is a wrong kind of question. These may seem like legitimate, harmless questions, but they are not. Your questions are answered by Infinite Intelligence through your built-in mental/spiritual system. Sooner or later, the answers show up AS your life. Here are some ideas to help you ask the right questions and to make a big, positive difference in the way you think and live.

First, identify your goals

What do you really want? Think of 3 or 4 desires and write them down on paper. Be brief. Do this *now*. Set them aside for a few minutes while you read the rest of this chapter.

How I learned about this exciting, powerful method

Several years ago, I was trying to publish my book, *How I CAN Have Everything!* but without success. I needed several thousand dollars and it just seemed to avoid me. Then one day, I received a small book in the mail with a letter from Linda S., a real nice lady in Colorado, who knew I was trying to publish my book. She said that she had demonstrated a new car in just two weeks after reading the book and doing as it instructs. She said that if I would read the book and follow the instructions in it, I would publish my book.

The book she sent to me was: *The Great Little Book of Afformations,"* by Noah St. John*. I immediately sat down and read it – twice! Then I made a list of Afformations, the first one pertaining to the publishing of my book, *How I CAN Have Everything.* The good news is that within six months, I did! Not only that, I soon published *Pro$per Now!* and I have demonstrated many other things such as a real nice home of my own and a new Toyota Prius Hybrid car. I am a believer! You will be too when you *do* as you are instructed here.

I have taught the Asking the Right Questions method to hundreds of people, individually in person and by phone, and in classes and workshops. Although it is presented here in short form, there is enough information for you to get started, and to produce delightful results.

*Noah St. John, director of *The Success Clinic Of America*, originated *The Afformations Method*. Contact him at: Successclinic.com

Do not under-estimate the power of asking the right questions!

Keep on with what works

It is important to know that asking the right questions does not take the place of prayer, meditation, or affirmations. Keep on with these practices because they help you to create a solid inner connection with the Source, causing you to grow spiritually, and putting a solid foundation under this process. Asking the right questions is an additional extremely powerful "tool" for achieving the things you really want. It's another wonderful way to truly live the more abundant life!

Most people ask wrong questions

As stated before, people often ask wrong, disempowering questions, and the answers show up AS their lives. Then they wonder why life doesn't treat them better.

Have you ever asked, "Why do I never have enough money?" "Why am I so unhappy?" "Why is it so hard for me to get along with other people?" "Why is it so hard for me to lose weight?" or similar questions?

Your I A M or
Infinite Answering Mechanism

When you ask any kind of question, which you do much more often than you might think, your I A M, Infinite Answering Mechanism, tries to find the answer to the question. Its only function is to try to find answers to whatever questions you ask, negative or positive, downgrading or uplifting. It cannot do otherwise. So the key to getting what you *want* instead of getting what you *don't* want, is to ask the *right questions*. In other words, change negative questions to positive questions. For instance:

Instead of asking, "Why do I never have enough money?" *ask:* "Why do I always have plenty of money?"

Instead of asking, "Why am I so unhappy?" *ask,* "Why am I so happy?"

Instead of asking, "Why is it so hard for me to get along with other people?" *ask,* "Why am I so loving and easy to get along with?"

Instead of asking, "Why is it hard for me to lose weight?" *ask,* "Why is it easy for me to always be at my right weight?"

If you want to sell your home, *instead of asking,* "Why can't I sell my home?" *ask,* "Why is my home now easily sold to the right party for the right price?"

Now look at the desires you wrote down. Formulate a positive question pertaining to the achieving of each desire. For instance, if your desire is a new home, *ask:* "Why am I now happily living in the home of my dreams?"

If your desire is a vacation, *ask:* "Why am I now enjoying a happy, relaxing and renewing vacation?"

For employment, *ask:* "Why am I now doing work I love and being generously paid?"

If your desire is to be financially free and independent, *ask,* "Why am I now financially free and independent?"

Ask the right questions over and over, with feeling, as though your desires are yours now. Asking right questions creates a feeling of already having. When you do ask them, you will quickly realize this is true.

You get the idea. Be alert! Listen to yourself. Change those negative, disempowering questions to positive, empowering questions. It will make you smile a lot!

HOW is not your concern!

Do *not* be concerned with *HOW* your financial increase will come, or *HOW* your loving companion will show up. Ask believing, and forget about *how*. The HOW is God's part. It is really a simple process. You ask right questions, your I A M goes to work, God provides the answers and they show up *as* your greatly improved life. Give no thought to *how*. Right questions are always in the present tense. "Now" is much more important than "How." "Why" is very important, because your *Infinite Answering Mechanism* works better with "Why?"

Change the preceding questions to suit your particular desires. Create your own questions. Ask them over and over as though you really want them answered, but do not answer them!

Jesus said that we do not get what we want because we ask amiss. He meant that we should ask right questions that are positive and in accord with what we really desire. He also said that when we pray, to BELIEVE we receive. I discovered that when I began to ask right questions, I got a wonderful feeling that what I was asking for was already mine. Right question asking is truly a very powerful action.

Passion is essential!

It is essential that you put a lot of passion into asking the right questions. It is the same kind of passion that you would express when you really want to be healed, or to make an important demonstration. When two people meet, it is passion that moves them into a closer, intimate relationship.

Sincerely ask your questions over and over and pay attention to the *feeling* that comes when you ask right, positive questions. It will probably be a happy feeling because you are asking as though it is already a done deal, which it is! Ask your right questions audibly, speaking them with feeling, or silently can be powerful, too. Sincerity is a key to success because you are asking questions which you honestly and definitely want answered.

It is helpful to put some variance into your questions. This means to ask them with different inflection in voice, and/or, putting emphasis on different words. When you are working on something you really, really want, you may need to ask the appropriate question many times a day. If so, do it! It's powerful to ask them just before going to sleep at night.

An important word is "NOW." When you ask a question, it is wise to include "Now." "Easy" or "Easily" are also helpful.

Extremely Important!

Do *NOT* answer any positive question you ask. That is *not* your job. Ask the question and let your built-in I A M, *Infinite Answering Mechanism,* do its job. When you ask a right, positive question enough times, *with feeling and sincerity,* like you really want an answer, the answer *must* show up as happy, positive changes in your life. There is no way that it cannot!

Asking the right questions will work for you when you work it. Do not underestimate the power of this action. Two people, I know, found very good jobs with excellent pay when they asked the right questions concerning employment. A married couple needed to sell their home rather quickly. On a Saturday evening, I taught them how to ask the right question for doing that. The following Tuesday, a couple visited their home, liked it, and bought it! Often asking the right questions works rather fast!

Ask, and you will receive!

As stated above, I have taught asking the right questions to hundreds of people, and it has worked for many of them, but not for everyone. The only reason it doesn't work is when a person stops asking, or they just don't use it. Do not be lazy, hazy or indifferent about this fabulous way to improve your life and manifest the things you really want. Give it a serious try for at least six months and I believe you will be pleasantly surprised at how easy and effective it is, and very happy with the results. It's simple! Refuse to ask wrong, negative questions, and insist upon asking only right, positive questions. Ask them over and over. It works when you work it. Please write and tell me about your success.

You can use asking right questions with your practice of multiplying your money. A question you might ask is: "Why is my tenfold return coming to me so easily?" Or, "Why am I giving freely and reaping a big harvest of multiplied money?" Formulate and ask your own questions.

When you are thinking about
doing something that stretches you financially,
do not think of the money as a loss;
instead, consider it an affirmation of
your worth or that of your project.

– Alan Cohen

16

Summary

You have every right to use money as seed, to bless other people with it and to make your tenfold claim on the amounts you give. This is a correct use of your mind and your money, especially when you act according to the spiritual laws and principles of prosperity.

With so much abundance in the world, there surely is plenty for you and for everyone. It is right that you claim and enjoy your fair share; to be abundantly supplied. You are wise, then, to do everything you can to prosper in the way that God desires for all of His children. When you do, you take a quantum leap upward into the more abundant life.

You, and all of us, are amazing little packages of light energy, the same energy that permeates everything in the Universe, and out of which all things are made. It makes us all one. Therefore what you do for yourself, you do for all.

Quantum prosperity requires a mutation or change—not just a little change—but a big one. The change, of course, must take place in your thinking before outer changes may be expected.

To experience the greater prosperity you desire, preparation is required. It is just like taking a long trip by car. You prepare your car, determine the route you will take, gather together materials, pack your bags and start off on your great adventure.

On your prosperity trip, you leave behind unnecessary baggage such as old, limiting ideas, poverty thinking and speaking, and other attitudes of mind that would keep you from enjoying your travels in Abundance Land. You relax, think and speak prosperously and enjoy your new wealth.

Non-resistance pays rich dividends. It is profitable to be non-resistant to the greater good God has for you. Let go of resistance to forgiving yourself and others. Accept that the Grace of God is yours and is given freely. All you need to do is to open yourself to it, claim and accept it for yourself. Grace is God's gift to you.

Love causes your prosperity to leap upward more easily and better than anything. Love is your great quantum prosperity power. It is good to affirm for prosperity and act in faith, but it is Love that fulfills your desires. Consider your love for prosperity. That which you love, tends to love you. Love is the highest frequency of the Law of Attraction, therefore, the most prospering.

Substance is always everywhere present. It is the "thinking stuff" out of which all things are made. Substance is never depleted. You may draw from it and use it as much as you possibly can and never use it all. Everything you see is the out-picturing of Substance. You shape and form Substance with your mind.

Substance cannot be limited and neither can you except in your thinking. You are wise to allow yourself to think expansively. You may take any size container to the ocean, dip it in and your container will be filled, but an infinite amount of water is left in the sea. The same is true with Substance. Take what you want and there is always more.

It is essential to have faith in Substance for out of it comes the fulfillment of the desires of your heart. Substance is the stuff that actually prospers you.

Thought is the power by which you create visible form out of Substance. Thought is creative. Thinking is the formulating process of your mind. You are wise to keep centered in God so that your thinking is clear and your purpose is true. This assures right results.

Prosperity is always *for* you. Accept this as Truth. Make sure the quality of your thinking matches the high quality and quantity of the prosperous life you desire. How determined are you to prosper? Keeping your desire and enthusiasm high will move you and your prosperity toward each other more quickly and magnificently.

Every thought-seed you allow to be sown in your mind produces after its kind. Rather than attracting to you, what you *want,* you attract to you what you *are* in consciousness. Thought is like a train. Trains deliver cargo. Make sure your thought-train is fueled by prosperity thoughts and delivers you to Abundance City.

Don't "Swiss Cheese" your prosperity with doubts and fears. Regardless of what other people may think or do, keep your thoughts and your faith centered in the allness of God and His ability to provide abundantly for you.

Allow your mind to think in grand terms. Would you rather live in a very small, confining environment like the frog in the well, or in an unlimited environment like the frog of the ocean? Your outer conditions are determined by your mental conditioning.

Money is wonderful! It deserves to be thought well of. Don't scare it away with despairing thoughts or feelings toward it. Love it for what it is: Divine Substance in handy, useable form, God's good green energy. Using money as seed in order to multiply it in your life enables you to enjoy more of the rich blessings God has for you. And, in so doing, you bless other people, too.

Money is neutral, alive energy and is yours to use. It is important to pay attention to your thoughts and feelings concerning it. Money always responds better to love, joy and positive thoughts and words. Remind yourself often that money is abundantly available. Believe that you are worthy of plenty of it; that you deserve as much as God has for you, which is limitless.

Get used to the idea of having plenty of money. You have decided to multiply your money, so expect to have much more of it flowing through your life. Because of reading this book and doing as it instructs, you are creating a larger stream of money. Gratefully, expect it to flow in and send it out in the same way.

Using money as seed is a very practical way to bless other people and to multiply your money as you do. Belief is the key to success. Do not let other people's doubts affect you. Sow money quietly, make your claim, and give thanks for the increase that is already yours. The Law of Tenfold return is based on faith; absolute trust in omnipresent Substance-Energy always surrounding you. Using money as seed multiplies like rabbits!

When you follow the Recipe for Multiplied Money, it works perfectly for you. Act as though it is already so. You are working with the Law of Giving and Receiving. It never fails when you work in harmony with it.

Look for opportunities to "plant" money-seed. The principle works the same with any amount. When you give someone a gift, or service, it is perfectly okay to make your tenfold claim on the value of that. This does not include your tithe, which should not be used as seed. The more you give and make your claim, the more you receive. Tithe on all you receive.

Gratitude is essential to living the abundant life. When you use the Recipe, your thanks is always toward God, the Source. Gratitude is love in expression and creates a closer, more open relationship with God. Thanksgiving keeps your consciousness centered in omnipresent Substance. Use your wonderful imagination to see your tenfold return coming to you and be just as grateful as you can be; just as though you already have it.

Mystic Nourishment is the very essence of Life. It is food for your soul, but it is not free. You must appropriate it and pay for it. Poverty is never God's will. You are here to live life just as richly as possible. Tithing is one of the best ways to connect with the Source. You are not obligated to tithe. But when you understand the Law of Giving and

Receiving, and know that God is the Source of your supply, you gratefully and faithfully tithe. When you tithe, you may be certain that you have God as your Partner. His resources are infinite!

Tithe means ten. It is 10% of your whole income given toward the spreading of spiritual truth on Mother Earth. The tithe is not a gift nor is it charity. It is paying for your spiritual food, Mystic Nourishment. Tithing brings joy and happiness that can be found in no other way because it keeps you and your finances connected to the Source.

Your true quest is to know God. This means to give time to quiet prayer and meditation in which you withdraw from worldly things and give your whole attention to God. Then you take this consciousness into everything you do. In God, there are no problems, no lack, nothing but love, life, joy, peace absolute-good. The more you identify with God within, the more wonderful your life is.

It is essential that you know what you want and to ask right or positive questions directly pertaining to your desires. If it is more money that you want, ask: "*Why is money now coming to me easily and abundantly?*" Ask similar "Why" questions for whatever you desire. *Never answer a question.* Leave that to your I A M *(Infinite Answering Mechanism)* and the Universe, which has all the answers and always responds accordingly. Do not be concerned with *HOW*. *How* is not your business. The Universe knows exactly *how* to answer your question. Let your *Infinite Answering Mechanism* and the Universe do what they do best. Your part is to ask right questions, relax, let go, and enjoy the answers that show up as your happier, more prosperous life.

All that is presented in this book is designed to give you a better connection with the Source, to use the spiritual Laws and Principles that govern life, and to enjoy the happy results. You deserve all the good that God has for you. Do your part and the results are automatic.

To enhance your understanding and practice of affirmative prayer, please refer to the author's book, *Positive Prayer. –* Over 100 Positive Prayers for improving every area of your life.

17

Conclusion

Thank you for reading this book. Now you have a clear understanding about prosperity and how to multiply your money. You will do well when you follow the Recipe for Multiplied Money and use money to bless others. Of special importance is the need to create a true spiritual foundation for wealth so that it is real and lasting. I suggest that you refer to this book often to help you keep on the right track – the express prosperity train track! Then you will breeze right on by Poverty Station headed for Abundance City!

Keep uppermost in mind that all the money in the world is not worth more than love. Love is by far the most important thing of all. It is the fulfilling energy of all of your desires. As good and wonderful as money is, love brings you joy that no amount of money can. When you give love, you give yourself, and you help bring peace and harmony to our world. Give love and the whole Universe gives all of Itself to you.

I wrote in my book, *BE What You Are: LOVE*, "*The imperative thing for life, for freedom and peace, is love. Love is the golden answer to everything.*"

The Universe wants you to prosper in a big way. Accept this as true and go for it with all your heart!

You will find all of my books inspiring and helpful.

John Wolcott Adams
P O Box 30989
AZ 85046 USA

RevJohn@GoldenKeyMinistry.com

A special word of thanks. - I am grateful for the many friends whose love and tithes helped me establish Golden Key Ministry-Unity and who financially support our Prayer Ministry. Thank you for your past financial giving and for all that you continue to give. I am grateful for the readers of my books who write to me and who give special tithes in support of my ministry. Thank you! You are loved and appreciated! – *John Wolcott Adams*

My record of multiplied money ...

My record of multiplied money ...

LaVergne, TN USA
13 August 2010
193177LV00003B/2/P